Praise for
The Camino Way

"*The Camino Way* offers universal life and leadership lessons. After finishing, I couldn't decide which I wanted to do first: share the book with my senior team or buy a plane ticket and start my own journey."

—Scott Kubly, Director of the
Seattle Department of Transportation

"Rooted in history, yet highly relevant today, Victor Prince's book takes readers on a journey of insight that can add value to all of our daily experiences."

—Suzanne Tager, Senior Director,
Retail and Consumer Goods Practice, Bain & Company

"Most people have two stacks of books by their bed: books they read for work, and books they read for pleasure. *The Camino Way* is the only book you'll read this year that could make it to both stacks."

—Paul Smith, bestselling author of
Lead with a Story and *Sell with a Story*

"*The Camino Way* takes you on a journey you will never forget. Awesome storytelling that captures and sweeps you in while delivering great life and leadership lessons. Another outstanding book from Victor Prince!"

—Brigette Hyacinth, Founder and Director of
the MBA Caribbean Organisation

Victor Prince not only shares valuable lessons and insights from his walk on the Camino, he goes one step further. Through his journey, he guides us to apply this newfound perspective to the most meaningful aspects of our lives. And, in doing so, we become better leaders, better parents, and better people."

—Sally Tassani, President, The Strategy Forums

"Let Victor Prince be your guide in this supremely engaging, lesson-packed breath of fresh air. Prince insightfully draws lessons in leadership embedded within the famed walk ranging from the power of living in each moment, to learning to ask for help, to ensuring to honor predecessors. If a "Buen Camino" is not on your itinerary, this book will bring you as close to the life-changing power of the vaunted walk as possible. It's like an MBA for the soul."

—Scott Mautz, author of *Find the Fire:*
Ignite Your Inspiration & Make Work Exciting Again

the
Camino
Way

the
Camino
Way

LESSONS IN LEADERSHIP FROM

A WALK ACROSS SPAIN

VICTOR PRINCE

AMACOM
American Management Association
New York · Atlanta · Brussels · Chicago · Mexico City · San Francisco
Shanghai · Tokyo · Toronto · Washington, D.C.

American Management Association: www.amanet.org
This publication is designed to provide accurate and authoritative information in regard
to the subject matter covered. It is sold with the understanding that the publisher is not
engaged in rendering legal, accounting, or other professional service. If legal advice or
other expert assistance is required, the services of a competent professional person
should be sought.

LIBRARY OF CONGRESS CATALOGING-IN-PUBLICATION DATA
Names: Prince, Victor, author.
Title: The Camino way : lessons in leadership from a walk across Spain /
by
  Victor Prince.
Description: New York, NY : AMACOM, [2017] | Includes bibliograph-
ical
  references and index.
Identifiers: LCCN 2017000715 (print) | LCCN 2017018021 (ebook) |
ISBN
  9780814438251 (E-book) | ISBN 9780814438244 (hardcover)
Subjects: LCSH: Leadership. | Camino de Santiago de Compostela.
Classification: LCC HD57.7 (ebook) | LCC HD57.7 .P7559 2017 (print)
| DDC
  658.4/092--dc23
LC record available at https://lccn.loc.gov/2017000715

About AMA
American Management Association (www.amanet.org) is a world leader in talent development, advancing the skills of individuals to drive business success. Our mission is
to support the goals of individuals and organizations through a complete range of
products and services, including classroom and virtual seminars, webcasts, webinars,
podcasts, conferences, corporate and government solutions, business books, and research. AMA's approach to improving performance combines experiential learning—
learning through doing—with opportunities for ongoing professional growth at every
step of one's career journey.

10 9 8 7 6 5 4 3 2 1

To José G. Valiño

Acknowledgments

THIS BOOK WAS MADE POSSIBLE BY THE SUPPORT OF MANY WONDER-
ful people. My heartfelt appreciation goes out to you all.

To all the people who live, work, and volunteer along the
Camino de Santiago—thank you for your kindness and support
to *peregrinos* (pilgrims).

To the nonprofit organizations supporting the Camino de
Santiago and *peregrinos*—thank you for all the work you do. To
help do my part, I commit to tithe a portion of my royalties
from this book to the American Pilgrims on the Camino, a nonprofit organization dedicated to that mission.

To my fellow *peregrinos* from around the world who were
kind enough to share their Camino stories with me for this
book: Adel from South Africa, Alain from France, Allan from
Australia, Andi from the USA, Anja from Denmark, Anja from
Germany, Anne from Australia, Antonella from Italy, Armi-
nelle from Australia, Bill from Canada, C. from Ireland, Carl
from Belgium, Carmen from Germany, Carol from the USA,
Chris from Canada, Chris from the USA, Christa from the USA,
Christopher from the UK, Christopher from the USA, Colm
from Ireland, Daniel from Spain, Donal from Ireland, Dave
from the USA, Deb from Australia, Deirdre from the USA,
Derek from Scotland, Dolores from Ireland, Edna from the
USA, Eileen from the USA, Eileen from the UK, Erik from the
USA, Felicity from the UK, Francesca from Italy, Gail from
Australia, Gemma from Ireland, Gerri from Australia, Grace

from the USA, Hans from Belgium, Jackie from the USA, James from the USA, Jo Anne from the USA, Joan from Ireland, Joann from the USA, Jodi from the USA, John from the USA, John from Ireland, John from the Netherlands, Jonathan from Ireland, Judith from Australia, Kailagh from New Zealand, Karen from the USA, Kat from the USA, Kathleen from the USA, Katie from the USA, Kenneth from Belgium, L. from Canada, Larry from Australia, Leah from the USA, Lorraine from Ireland, Lysa from England, Marc from the USA, Marianne from Ireland, Mario from Germany, Maryanne from the USA, Maryjane from the USA, Michael from Ireland, Michelle from Canada, Oihana from Ireland, Ondrej from the Czech Republic, Pam from the USA, Patrick from the USA, Pearl from New Zealand, Peter from the Netherlands, Pierre from Germany, Raine from New Zealand, Roberta from Canada, Rose from South Africa, Rosie from Australia, Sandy from the USA, Shannon from Canada, Shelley from the USA, Sophie from France, Stefanie from Germany, Stephen from England, Steve from Ireland, Steve from the USA, Tammy from the USA, Tania from Canada, TC from Germany, Terry from England, Tiera from Hawaii, "Texas" Tim from the USA, Tina from Sweden, Tony from California, Trevor from the UK, Valerie from Canada, Wendy from Australia, and Wijnand from the Netherlands. After reading your stories, I felt like I had met each of you on the *meseta* and our conversation made us both forget the heat and blisters. Thank you for sharing part of your Camino with me.

To Mom and Dad—for everything.

To Tina—for the support and inspiration that make me a better writer and man.

To Team Prince—for all the help clearing the way for me to write the book I kept telling you about.

To My Camino Family from the USA, the UK, Ireland,

Belgium, New Zealand, Sweden, Canada, Germany, and France—for sharing your Camino with me.

To Giles Anderson—for being my favorite literary agent.

To Anne Prince—for research assistance on this book.

To Stephen S. Power, Timothy Burgard, and the AMACOM team—for taking a chance on me and for making this book the best it could be.

To Miranda Pennington, Phil Gaskill, and the Neuwirth and Associates team—for excellent editing and production work.

To Mike Figliuolo—for teaching me how to turn an idea into a book.

To the Indianapolis Museum of Art, the Indianapolis Art Center, and Karlstads Universitets bibliotek—for providing me with inspiring and productive spaces to write this book.

To The Fellas, The Four Amigos, The Brotherhood, The Gang—for many years, and many years to come, of friendship.

To all my friends, family, colleagues, and neighbors who asked me at some point how "The Book" was coming along—writing a book is a lonely, uncharted trek with no guaranteed finish line. Even the smallest gestures of interest and support meant more than you realized.

Contents

Introduction

"Halfway along our journey to life's end
I found myself astray in a dark wood,
Since the right way was nowhere to be found."

—OPENING LINE OF DANTE'S *INFERNO*

I PEDALED ONE LAST TIME AND COASTED AS LONG AS I COULD. WHEN I stopped, I was staring across the Danube River at the stunning Hungarian Parliament building. After a month, my "bucket list" bicycle trip across the heart of Europe was over. I felt exhausted. I felt closure. I also felt that something was missing.

My childhood-self had set two goals for my life—to be president and to see the world. The failure to see the overlap between the two belied my naïveté. Somewhere between childhood in the Midwest and college in Washington, DC, I realized I was never going to be president. I decided I would settle for one rung down the public-service career ladder—running a federal agency. Even before graduating from college, I got a great government job and had a precocious start climbing the ladder. My colleagues even nicknamed me "Doogie" after a popular television character at the time who was a teenage doctor. As I worked with the leaders of government, I realized that they often got to the top by having successful business careers first and turning to public service later. So I left government to go to business school and start a new career. My business career went well but didn't fully inspire me, so after several years I went back to public service. I became a cabinet member for the mayor of a large city and then the Chief Operating Officer (COO) of a federal government agency.

I'd reached one rung below my college goal and realized that was as far as I wanted to go. Federal government had changed a lot since I set my goal, so I considered that career box checked.

I was in my mid-forties. The feeling was both satisfying and disconcerting. What do you do after you check off your career goal before your career is over?

I focused on my second teenage goal—to see the world. As a kid, my parents gave me a globe and a suitcase as Christmas gifts. Scientists would identify a "wanderlust" gene years later, but my parents must have diagnosed me early. By my mid-forties, I had lived in ten cities and traveled across four continents. I never let relocation get in the way of career advancement, even if it stunted my life outside of my career.

Along the way, I got addicted to long-distance biking trails as the best way to experience travel. I loved the idea of traveling with a goal—get from one village to another, go across a state, go across a country. I biked many trails. From Pittsburgh to Washington, DC. From Montreal to Quebec City. Across New York State on the Erie Canal. I did a lot of long trails, but only ones that met three criteria: they sounded impressive to complete, they didn't require camping, and they fit into a normal vacation time for work.

Now that I was taking a career sabbatical, I could do a trail that took longer than a week. The Danube River bike trail scored perfectly against my criteria. Covering about fifty miles per day on a bike, I would see a lot of Europe. It had places to stay and eat all along the way. And because it followed a river, it was flat. It was perfect.

But as I admired the unexpected beauty of Budapest, I felt more empty than fulfilled. My month of biking had been the loneliest month I'd ever spent. Every night was in a different village or city. It's not easy to have conversations with people as you speed by on a bike. Biking is a great way to see the sights, but it's not a good way to meet people.

I'd wanted solitude as part of my sabbatical. Over my career, I'd led progressively larger teams. The COO job I just left had me leading a team of hundreds of people. I loved leading teams and developing people, but, after two decades, my batteries needed some alone time to recharge.

I started looking for another trail as soon as I got home from Budapest. I decided to hike instead of bike this time, to get a more social experience.

I was surprised at how few trails there are in the world that you can hike for thirty days without camping. The one trail that kept topping the list was the Camino de Santiago pilgrimage trail across Spain. For more than a thousand years, pilgrims (*peregrinos* in Spanish) walked hundreds of miles to reach the cathedral in Santiago de Compostela, Spain, to see the shrine built for the remains of St. James.

The Camino was great for a results-driven Type-A personality like me. Every night, I had to punch a stamp to show that I had succeeded that day. If I got enough stamps, I got a certificate at the end. How had I not already done this trail? It was perfect.

The Camino was the clear choice from my list, but the religious roots of the trail gave me pause. My research, though, told me the Camino was as religious or nonreligious as hikers made it. I pieced together an itinerary, packed everything I would need for a month in my backpack, and flew to Spain.

The next thirty days on the Camino ended up being the best adventure I'd ever embarked on. More important than the beautiful scenery, history, and great company I had expected was how my eyes were opened.

I found insight and inspiration, but not just on the "finding myself" front like many *peregrinos*. Many of the insights were about the thing I do when I am not on vacation—leading people at work.

I've learned a lot about leadership in my career. By earning a Master in Business Administration (MBA) at the Wharton School of the University of Pennsylvania, I learned about the theory and history of leadership at work. As a consultant, I've been able to work with leaders in a wide variety of industries and countries. As an executive, I've led people across a wide set of functions, including human capital, finance, facilities, purchasing, project management, information technology, and customer contact centers. And, like most everyone, I've had a lot of bosses to learn from as well.

The Camino provided a new, unexpected laboratory for me to learn about leadership. Every day presented new challenges that I had to manage through. I met dozens of hikers from around the world and got to learn about their careers.

The Camino also provided time for inner reflection. The many social moments with other hikers were separated by long stretches of alone time. I found myself recalling interactions and decisions I had made over my last several years of work, and my mind focused on what I wished I could redo. I started to imagine how I would have done things differently if I'd had the benefit of the Camino lessons I was now learning.

After I got home, I started writing about those insights and shared them on my blog about strategy and leadership. Each blog entry described how different experiences on the Camino taught me new leadership lessons or reinforced old ones in new ways. Those blogs went viral. They hit a wellspring with thousands of people from around the world who have done, or aspire to do, adventures like the Camino. They also resonated with people looking for new ways to learn about traditional management disciplines. Many readers encouraged me to write a book. Their support convinced me that there would be an audience. The confidence boost I got by completing my Camino convinced me that I could take on a new adventure—writing this book.

PART I

MEETING THE CAMINO

CHAPTER 1

The History of
the Camino de Santiago

IN THE FIRST HALF OF THE NINTH CENTURY, A SPANISH BISHOP NAMED Teodomiro decided to investigate reports of strange lights and sounds coming from a hill in the northwest of Spain. After climbing the hill, the bishop discovered a site with three tombs, and he declared one of them to be the remains of St. James (*Santiago* in Spanish), one of the twelve disciples of Jesus.[1] According to the Camino legend, Jesus tasked his disciples with going out to different parts of the world and spreading their new faith. James went to Spain; he later returned to Judea and was killed by the local authorities. His associates put his body, by itself, in a boat in the Mediterranean Sea. The boat drifted to the coast of the northwest corner of Spain, where it washed up onshore, covered in scallop shells. Locals found the boat and buried the remains on a nearby hill. That burial site was what the bishop Teodomiro declared he had discovered about 800 years later.[2] To celebrate, the king ordered a small church to be built on the site over the tomb.[3] Word about the discovery spread, and people started to visit the shrine. In the year 950, an intrepid bishop named Gotescalc from LePuy, France traveled 800 miles to see the shrine "to beg mercy and help from God and Santiago," becoming the first pilgrim to be recorded as visiting the site.[4]

To understand how the Camino de Santiago developed after that first pilgrim, it helps to understand how other pilgrimages cut a path through European history before the Camino. Even in pre-Roman-Empire times, the custom existed of visiting hallowed places to get spiritual help.[5] Individuals from Europe probably started pilgrimages to Jerusalem and the Christian-history sites (the "Holy Land") as early as the second or third century.[6] By the fourth century, pilgrimage to the Holy Land was probably an established concept, with the Bible as a guide-book.[7]

Once the concept of Christian pilgrimage became established, a new destination for pilgrims arose to compete by the eighth century—Rome. As the capital of the growing Catholic Church, Rome offered its own religious sights-to-see as a draw, in addition to Roman Empire ruins. The spread of the Catholic Church to northern Europe around that time likely created a natural flow of people to and from the church's capital city.[8] In addition to Rome's draw, it was also an easier destination than the Holy Land for European pilgrims. It was both closer and under Christian control. The network of old roads originally built to connect the Roman Empire territories back to Rome probably helped, too.

The rise of the pilgrimage to Rome helped popularize the concept of pilgrimage. Even if few people would ever do a pilgrimage themselves, more would know what pilgrimage was. References to "pilgrims" started appearing in historical documents.[9] Rome and Tours, France, were mentioned as pilgrimage destinations and people were reported believing pilgrimage was a way to forgive their sins.[10] Pilgrims were recognized for their distinctive appearance with their clothing and equipment.[11] The pilgrim "brand" had been born.

In addition to pilgrims, Rome got some very unwelcome visitors in the year 846 in the form of a large Arab raiding party that sacked the city.[12] This was the latest in a series of attacks from Arabs in the south that made the people of Rome feel uneasy.[13] Rome must certainly have become a less attractive pilgrimage destination as a result.

The discovery of Santiago's remains was declared sometime around, but before, the year 842. (The king who ordered the building of the first church on the spot died in 842.)[14] The timing was fortuitous. Just as the concept of pilgrimage had become established, one of its biggest destinations—Rome—was becoming less attractive. In addition, that northern area of Spain had pushed back the Muslim invaders in the century before.[15] Getting a stream of Christian visitors was also probably helpful in keeping the Muslims at bay.[16]

The century between the building of the first shrine to St. James's remains and the first recorded pilgrim to the site (that of Gotescalc in the year 950) was an eventful time. It was the heart of the "Viking Age" in Europe, gunpowder was used in battle for the first time in China, and the Mayan Empire was collapsing in the "undiscovered" Americas. In the northwest corner of Spain, religious and royal officials were working hard to promote their area as a new pilgrimage destination. The small church at the shrine was replaced by a bigger one in 899.[17] King Ramiro I ordered people to pay a tribute to the church in Santiago.[18] Ramiro's grandson, King Alfonso III, sent a letter in 906 to the clergy in Tours (a pilgrimage site itself) in response to their questions about this new shrine, demonstrating that word about the shrine was spreading.[19]

The next two centuries (c. 950–c. 1150) were eventful, with the Norman conquest of England, the first European crusade to retake Jerusalem, the founding of the first universities (Bologna and Oxford), and Leif Erikson's landing in modern-day Canada. In the northwest corner of Spain, more pilgrims were coming to see the shrine to Santiago, and the locals were building infrastructure to support them. As the local Christian kings in Spain pushed out the Moors, they left behind roads and castles built to support those military efforts.[20] A new basilica (the Cathedral of Santiago de Compostela) was started in 1075 and new settlements emerged among the pilgrim roads, such as Puente de la Reina, founded in 1090.[21]

In addition to physical infrastructure, local church officials, particularly Bishop Don Diego Gelmírez (1100–1139), were laying religious groundwork for a pilgrim superhighway. Gelmírez successfully lobbied Rome to get the right to grant indulgences and remissions of sins, in those years in which the feast of St. James (July 25) fell on a Sunday.[22] Because indulgences were typically only granted in Rome, this made Santiago even more attractive as a pilgrimage destination.

The final piece of Camino infrastructure that emerged in this time was an innovation—the travel guide. Around the year 1140, a compilation of documents about the miracles of St. James and the pilgrimage to his shrine emerged out of Santiago. It came to be known as the Codex Calixtinus, named after Pope Calixtus II (1121–1124), a pope Bishop Gelmírez had successfully lobbied.[23] Beyond the religious content, one part of the Codex centered on describing Santiago as a destination, the routes to get there, and logistical information on the way.[24] It even made the earliest known reference to the souvenir trade in the Christian West.[25]

A lot happened in the four centuries between the emergence of the Codex Calixtus and the start of the Protestant Reformation (1517). Christopher Columbus, Marco Polo, Johannes Gutenberg, and William "Braveheart" Wallace all lived in this time. In the northwest corner of Spain, the combination of indulgences and the Codex Calixtus were turning Santiago de Compostela into a top pilgrimage destination. Pilgrims started appearing from England before the close of the twelfth century.[26] In the fifteenth century, interest in Santiago had spread further, with records of pilgrimage to Santiago starting to appear from individual travelers from Italy, France, England, Germany, Sweden, and Poland.[27, 28] Amazingly, this period of growth included two tragic stages in European history—the Black Death plague (1340s) and the Hundred Years War (1337–1453).

The recorded reasons for pilgrimage are scarce, but the stories that did survive center on the need to get sins forgiven—voluntarily or involuntarily. After the murder of Thomas Becket in 1170, for example, English king Henry II promised to make a pilgrimage as penance for his role, and he asked the pope to choose between Rome, Jerusalem, and Santiago as his destination.[29]

Some pilgrimages were not to ask forgiveness, but to ask for relief. Between 1456 and 1483, for example, four separate cities in Spain, Italy, and France sent representatives to Santiago to beg for help in lifting plagues from their cities.[30]

Some pilgrimages may have had less spiritual reasons. Some trips were probably as much for tourism as religion, like a German party of 1387 who admitted as much in their safe-passage letter.[31] And, as always, some pilgrimages may have had anything but spiritual reasons, such as running away from the law or from servitude.[32]

How many pilgrims were there during this peak age of the Camino de Santiago? There are no reliable statistics on pilgrims reaching Santiago, but a few points of data might give a sense of scale. A narrative from an Italian pilgrim in the 1600s mentioned that the Royal Hospice in Roncesvalles fed "up to thirty-thousand pilgrims a year," a number that sounds more like hyperbole than statistics, but may help set an upper-bound sense of the scale of pilgrims at the time.[33] A register of the Hospital de la Reina for the year 1594 logged 16,767 pilgrims, an average of about 45 per day, and on some days they had more than 200.[34]

Whatever the number of pilgrims during this golden age, it must have been only a fraction of the hundreds of thousands per year that are recorded now. For example, the estimated 3,600 pilgrims that came from England during the entire 14th century is less than the number that come from the United Kingdom in one year now (5,417 in 2015).[35, 36] Any annual number of pilgrims in the thousands during the twelfth through fifteenth centuries should still be considered impressive, given the challenges of travel and the much smaller total population of Europe.

Pilgrimage on the Camino started to decline in the 16th century.[37] Other methods than pilgrimage to get indulgences had emerged a century earlier.[38] The Protestant Reformation further knocked down the reputation of indulgences.

Part of the decline of pilgrimage on the Camino probably arose from its popularity as well. Records from the beginning of the period suggest that some poor people began using the system of pilgrim hospices not for pilgrimage, but more as the equivalent of modern homeless shelters.[39] While the number of pilgrims was decreasing, the costs of supporting the hospices built for the larger crowds of pilgrims of previous centuries remained. Hospices were selling off land to meet their operating costs in the 18th century, and many closed, or were destroyed, in the Napoleonic Wars.[40]

The Camino was still alive enough in 1779 for future US president John Adams to remark in his diary, during a trip across Spain to France along part of the route: "Upon the Supposition that this is the place of the Sepulture of Saint James, there are great numbers of Pilgrims, who visit it, every Year, from France, Spain, Italy and other parts of Europe, many of them on foot."[41]

Pilgrimage to Santiago never died out completely, but only about seventy pilgrims were thought to have traveled the route in 1979.[42] Then an old trick seems to have started a rebirth—a new Camino travel guide. Elías Valiña Sampedro, a priest in a town along the Camino, published the final version of *El Camino de Santiago, Guia del Pilgrim* in 1985, and it became a model for future guides.[43] Just as with the emergence of the Codex Calixtinus 800 years before, once a guidebook hit the market, people started coming.

Once pilgrims started coming, pilgrims started writing narratives, as they had hundreds of years before. Between 1985 and 1995, more than a dozen pilgrimage narratives were published in English.[44] The Brazilian writer Paulo Coelho published his own book about the Camino in 1987, a year before his blockbuster book, *The Alchemist*, was published. In 2000, Shirley MacLaine, a famous American film actress, published her own Camino narrative, which became a *New York Times* best seller. A German pilgrim's narrative in 2006 became a best seller in Germany. The 2010 film about the Camino called *The Way*, starring Martin Sheen and Emilio Estevez, seems to have been a key factor in increasing awareness of the Camino in the USA: since that film came out, requests for an American Camino credential have quadrupled from about 1,600 in 2010 to about 6,400 in 2015.[45] Pilgrims from other countries point to other recent books or films as their inspiration to walk the Camino. In short, the Camino de Santiago is officially back as it approaches its 1300th birthday.

Eleven centuries after that first recorded pilgrimage, in the year 2013, I was one of 215,880 people from all over the world who were recorded as pilgrims to the same shrine.[46] The small church had grown to be a great cathedral in Santiago de Compostela, a Spanish city of about 100,000 people that had grown around the shrine. My fellow pilgrims and I had walked roughly the same path the first pilgrims took, now known collectively in Spanish as *El Camino de Santiago*—the Path of Santiago.

CHAPTER 2

The Spirit of
the Camino

A Camino Pilgrim Credential — aka "Pilgrim Passport"

THE CAMINO BEGINS WITH ONE DOCUMENT AND ENDS WITH ANOTHER. Before starting their journey, pilgrims get a Pilgrim's Credential, informally known as a pilgrim, or *peregrino,* passport. I received my pilgrim passport from the nonprofit group that supports peregrinos from the US—American Pilgrims on the Camino. That credential serves two practical purposes. It identifies travelers to the low-cost hostels along the way that are only open to pilgrims. That helps the hostels keep out non-pilgrims looking for cheap accommodations. The passport is also where a pilgrim collects stamps at each stop along the way to prove his/her journey. Each hostel has a unique stamp with its name, location, and sometimes a logo. By adding a date to their stamp, the hostels can enforce policies to move pilgrims on after a day or two to make room for new pilgrims.

Upon arriving at the end of the trail in Santiago, pilgrims take their stamp-filled Credential to get the other bookend on a Camino—the Compostela certificate. Written in Latin, the Compostela is the certificate to show that a pilgrim has walked at least the last hundred kilometers of the trail. An official in the Oficina del Peregrino (Office of Pilgrims) from the Santiago de Compostela cathedral reviews each pilgrim's passport and asks for the starting point and the reason for the journey. The official then writes the pilgrim's name and date completed in Latin and hands it to the pilgrim with a final, official "Buen Camino."

I will always remember my trip to that office. It was part of a bittersweet day. I was elated that I had reached my goal but sad that my journey was over. I could sense similar emotions from other pilgrims' faces in line. Some of those faces were familiar; many were unfamiliar. All pilgrims from every Camino route into Santiago de Compostela converge at that office on the final day. When I finally got my Compostela certificate, my first thought was that I didn't know my first name had a Latin form, *Victorem*. My second thought was how to protect my priceless new document until it was on my wall at home.

If my house were on fire and I could only rescue one document, I would choose my crumpled and messy Credential over my Compostela certificate. The Compostela certificate reminds me that I succeeded in the challenge of walking across Spain. But my pilgrim passport reminds me of every step I took along the way to earn that certificate. The Camino is an example of the saying "the journey is its own reward," and the passport is like a record of the journey.

The process of getting a stamp as you check in for the night at the end of every day's walk is a ritual core to every *peregrino's* experience. Just as the sound of a gavel marks the close of many ceremonies, the thump of a stamp marks the close to each day on the Camino. For a results-driven executive like me, it was a form of immediate gratification on this adventure travel. Another day done—thump!

I remember getting my first stamp. I was excited, so I took a "selfie" picture. I bet most modern pilgrims do that too. I remember being overeager the rest of that first day hiking, getting a stamp at every rest or food break. As I admired my collection of stamps that night over dinner, I realized that I was going to run out of room for stamps if I kept up that pace. From then on, I held myself to just one at check-in each afternoon.

It took me a few days to realize that the real gift on that passport was not my budding collection of stamps, but rather the printing on the back. I had skimmed that writing when I first got my passport in the mail, but it had not made an impact on me. Now that I was on the trail, the words did make an impact. Under the title "Spirit of the Camino" were seven simple reminders of things pilgrims should do while on the Camino. I was struck by the combination of simplicity and depth in the words:

1. Welcome Each Day, Its Pleasures and Its Challenges

2. Make Others Feel Welcome

3. Share

4. Live in the Moment

5. Feel the Spirit of Those Who Have Come Before You

6. Appreciate Those Who Walk with You Today

7. Imagine Those Who Will Follow You

These reminders weren't religious. They just seemed like useful, commonsense things every leader should demonstrate every day. Reading them made me realize that I had not been doing all of them well in my personal and professional lives.

Even though I was walking a pilgrimage trail, I didn't consider myself a pilgrim. I was not looking for some revelation at the end of the trip. The most I was looking for was the ability to brag that I had walked across a country. I wanted to put another big adventure-travel trophy up on my wall.

Reading those principles made me realize that that was not going to be the purpose of my trip. This wasn't just going to be an epic summer adventure-travel vacation: this was going to be remedial summer school. I was going to be doing an intensive makeup for these seven simple leadership lessons that I'd failed to learn in business school, or had forgotten.

PART II

LEARNING FROM
THE CAMINO

A trail marker along the Camino de Santiago.

CHAPTER 3

Welcome Each Day, Its Pleasures and Its Challenges

IT TOOK ME FIFTEEN MINUTES TO REMOVE ALL THE THISTLES WEDGED into my hiking socks and pants. The trail wound through delicate fields of asparagus and somehow I'd found bad stuff in which to get stuck. Three English guys I'd passed earlier stopped to ask if I was all right. I told them my pride was injured but I wasn't, so they smiled and walked on. I'd end up telling them the story over beers that night.

The story started the previous night when I read a quote from another pilgrim that gave me an epiphany: "In the hospices you can have everything you want, except in the Hospital de Santiago: there the people are very mocking. The women in the hospice yell at the pilgrims a lot. But the food is good."[1] The content of the quote wasn't what moved me; it was the fact that the quote came from the journal of a German named Künig von Vach who had walked the Camino over *five hundred* years ago. I realized the pleasures and challenges I was facing were not that different from his. Like him, I had to learn to welcome both. The thistles in my pants were a challenge. The connection I felt with a pilgrim from centuries before was a pleasure. My excursion off the Camino path to explore the ruins of a centuries-old hostel had given me both.

As I interviewed dozens of other pilgrims while writing this book, I realized they also learned to welcome both pleasures and challenges each day on the Camino. For Hans, a consultant from Belgium, for example, "Every day felt great even when it was not. . . . Pleasures and challenges were not extremes anymore but a blur of emotions. I welcomed the whole mix." Erik, a father from the USA, "had to be mindful of each step with my one foot [which was] not blistered to the point of incredible pain. I learned to 'drink in' when I stepped on the 'good' foot." Domenico Laffi, an Italian pilgrim on the Camino in the 1600s, summed up a day of pleasures and challenges on the Camino this way in his journal: "Here we were hit by a very violent storm, with wind and rain, which left us almost dead. But it was followed by a very hot sun, which dried our clothes. So we kept going through the hills."[2]

When I first heard of the Camino Pilgrim value "Welcome Each Day, Its Pleasures and Its Challenges," it gave me an image of an attractive person in pajamas waking up, stretching, and opening a window to let in the morning sun and breeze. It made me want a coffee. Only after I got into a rhythm on the Camino did this mean more to me than a reminder of countless coffee commercials. I began to see each day not as just a unit of time dividing a week or month, but as an experience in itself. Every day on the Camino feels like a week because so many different experiences are packed into each one. I learned to welcome each day in a meaningful way. By getting into the practice on the Camino, I learned that this could be useful for my work-life after the Camino.

Welcome Each Day with a Reasonable Goal

Walking hundreds of miles across Spain is an intimidating goal. Pilgrims learn to break that big goal into smaller pieces. Anne, a psychiatrist from Australia, summed up her approach this way: "You only ever had to think of the day ahead, because the whole task was too great. Now I apply this to my writing—one page a day eventually ends in a book." Rosie, a personal assistant from Australia, learned to start the day with a simple goal: "Each morning we would say a little prayer about who we would meet that day, who we would be able to help along the way, and who would help us along the way. I still think this in my head every morning and try to help someone every day, even if it is just something small."

Before the Camino, I had an intimidating job. As a COO, I was ultimately responsible for all of the goals in my department. That meant I had to keep track of dozens of streams of activity aimed at those goals. Each project, program, initiative, or other activity had its own schedule and success metrics. To keep up, my days had me running through a calendar full of meetings, each one on a different area. Each day was like juggling a different set of balls. I found it hard to switch focus from one area to another in each meeting. I worried about things falling through the cracks. At the end of each day, I would feel like I had done my best, but I wasn't sure whether that day had been a success or not. All I knew was I had another day just like it lined up for tomorrow.

Walking the Camino across Spain was one of the most strenuous months of my life, and one of the most relaxing. The strenuous part was physical—walking fifteen miles a day for a month with a heavy backpack. The relaxing part was mental— the simplicity of life on the Camino. My destination was clear. My path to get there was well marked. Everything I needed was on my back.

I walked for a while one morning on the trail with a man named Salvador from Brazil. Like me, his walking pace was faster than average on the Camino. Unlike me, however, he was planning to finish the trail in three weeks versus my four. He was averaging many more miles per day than I was. That meant he spent almost all of his waking hours walking. It also meant he had to camp often, since he had little slack in his schedule to build it around towns. We were on the same path, headed to the same destination, but we were on different Caminos. He got little of the social part of the Camino that I got after each day of walking. His Camino was all about reaching his goal as quickly as he could.

I thought about our two Caminos as an analogy for my career. My career early on had been like his Camino. I had a destination—a "successful career"—and wanted to get there as quickly as possible. I competed with my peers. Hours worked and money banked were like points on a scoreboard. My workdays left little room for much of a life outside the office. Staying late at the office became more of a habit than a necessity. I lost sight of the fact that my career was a means to an end: a "successful life," not an end itself.

After I got back from the Camino, I decided to focus on one goal each day at work. When I achieved that goal, I would move on to enjoy life outside of work. Some days, my goal would be writing a thousand words in the manuscript for my next book. Some days, it would be to write a blog. Some days, it would be to update one of my websites. By choosing one thing to focus on each day, I have been able to focus better. With one simple goal, I get the feeling of accomplishment when I achieve that goal. Instead of moving an inch forward on each of several different fronts, I get the satisfaction of crossing a goal line every day, which is a great self-motivation tool.

CAMINO LESSON—
WELCOME EACH DAY WITH A REASONABLE GOAL.

▸ *Set a Reasonable Daily Range*—When I set my daily average goal for my Camino, I based it on how many hours I wanted to walk, not how many miles I could walk. If I had to keep walking past dinner, I was doing something wrong. It meant I'd gotten a late start, was taking too many breaks, or wasn't walking fast enough. The same goes for work. Set a cutoff time you have to work within. If you work late, address that as a failure, not as a point of pride. Remind yourself that it is important to have a balanced life between work and home. More importantly, people who work for you may be following your lead. People often think it looks bad to leave before the boss does, even if they don't need to be working late.

▸ *Define a "Win" for the Day at Work*—Look at your calendar each morning, or the night before, and think about what will make you feel like you have succeeded at the end of the day. If one of your meetings would help you resolve a big problem or achieve a big goal, figure out what outcome you want from that meeting. Make that your "win" for the day. If you have something you have been procrastinating, make starting it a goal one day. If you have a deliverable you need to get done that week, set completing it as a goal that day. Give yourself one clear goal that you can check off that day to make you feel like you are making progress on your larger journey.

Celebrate the Small Pleasures

Pilgrims learn the importance of celebrating the small pleasures on the Camino. The Camino can be a brutal grind physically. Celebrating the small pleasures builds a store of good energy to get you through challenges.

Pearl, an office manager from New Zealand, shared her lessons from the Camino this way: "On the Camino we would look at the map to see where we had to go that day, and if there were hills we thought: okay, just take one step at a time. Once out there, we never looked forward to see how far to go, which mountain to climb, or which path it might lead us on. We would walk and enjoy each village and new piece of scenery, then turn and look to see where we had come from and celebrate the big climb, or the fact that we were halfway up the mountain and how far we could now see."

Jo Anne, a pilgrim from the USA, shared her story about the importance of celebrating the small pleasures. "There were times on the Camino that I was overwhelmed. . . . I missed my husband, children, and grandchildren. After ten days or so, I sent a note to my son just saying that I was having a difficult time. . . . He sent me back the most beautiful, amazing note. Basically saying to stop and appreciate what I was doing. To stop acting as if the Camino was a race because the map said to go from point A to point B. My son told me to stop every day and sit at a café and have a cup of tea."

In my consulting days, I was not good at celebrating the small pleasures. I flew to client sites most every week. The travel time was on top of the high workload. If I had breakfast at all, it was probably something I grabbed from the hotel lobby and ate in a cab. If I had lunch, it was probably just a takeout eaten back in the team room, lest the clients think we were not working. Dinner was often the same—me, eating room service alone back at the hotel. Eating was nothing more than satisfying a biological need.

One night while working for a client in Detroit, I decided to treat myself to dinner at the seafood restaurant by the hotel. It was a Tuesday night in November, so it wasn't crowded. I sat alone at the bar and saw a group at a table in the back corner. When two of them got up to walk to the bathroom together, I realized why they were set apart from the rest. It was Stevie Wonder and his entourage. Upon hearing us call out to him, Mr. Wonder was kind enough to perform three songs on a piano about fifteen feet from my seat. What a way to end a day! That private concert made me wonder what I had been missing by not going out for dinner more.

That private concert also made me appreciate my work in a new way. Work as a consultant was giving me the chance to travel all over the United States and Europe. How many other interesting experiences that came with that travel had I failed to enjoy? I'd viewed consulting as my dream job coming out of business school. Now I was living it, but I wasn't appreciating everything it offered. I wasn't celebrating the opportunity to experience a piece of my dream job every day.

Each day on the Camino was a routine of everyday tasks separated by hours of walking. Every morning, I would start hiking before I had breakfast, trying to get a decent amount of the day's distance done before stopping. When I did find the first place to have a coffee, it was a reason to celebrate. The coffee represented a toast to my success in rising early and walking before breakfast. I had the same goal with lunch. I wanted to be done with more than half of my distance for the day before I stopped for lunch. Lunch became a celebration of achieving that goal. Dinner was usually the highlight of my day. It was a celebration of achieving my goal for that day, usually with other pilgrims.

I continued that routine after I got home from the Camino. Breakfast became more than my morning meal; it became a reward for getting my morning fitness workout done. Lunch became more than my midday meal; it became a celebration for having gotten off to a good start for my goal for the day. Dinner became more than my last meal of the day; it became a celebration for reaching my goal for the day. By tying all these rituals to some achievement, I learned to appreciate them more.

CAMINO LEADERSHIP LESSON—
CELEBRATE THE SMALL PLEASURES.

▸ *Use Breakfast as a Goal*—If you have something you want to do every morning, like exercising or getting through the newspapers, complete it first and treat breakfast as your reward.

▸ *Use Lunch Breaks as a Midpoint Deadline*—If you make good progress on your daily goal by lunchtime, reward yourself by treating your lunch as a small celebration.

▸ *Celebrate the Day's End*—If you complete your goal for the day, declare victory and focus on your life outside work for the rest of the day.

Put Challenges into Perspective

For many pilgrims, the Camino is one of the most challenging experiences in their life. By working through many difficulties every day, a pilgrim learns to put challenges into perspective. The Camino taught Bill, a pilgrim from Canada, this way: "I was alone without a guidebook or maps and my bank card was not working. Other pilgrims befriended me along The Way, and I learned that things generally work out, perhaps not the way that you think they will." The Camino made Peter, an executive coach from the Netherlands, "more relaxed and aware that everything will work out. Less anxious about possible outcomes. 'The Camino will provide.'" Stephen, a retired information technology specialist from England, "learnt to be calm about anything life throws and roll with it. Before, I would overthink situations and eventually get stressed. Didn't like changes to planned schedules. Now I have learnt to accept that it's life and simply smile."

Long before my Camino, I took on a big challenge by going to graduate school full-time to get my MBA degree in my mid-twenties. Two years forgoing a salary plus big tuition and other expenses meant I had put myself deep into debt. It was a huge bet on myself. When I got a job offer from a great consulting firm several months before I graduated, I was overjoyed. It was a perfect launching pad for a successful career in business. And just as importantly, it would enable me to pay off my debts.

When I started at the consulting firm, I wanted to make a great first impression. I was part of a cohort of about twenty other newly minted MBAs starting in my office that summer. Being competitive, I wanted to immediately stand out from the crowd.

For my first assignment, a manager asked me if I knew how to do variance analysis. I remembered hearing about that type of sophisticated analysis in one of my MBA classes. I didn't re-member doing it, but I knew I could figure it out. Besides, there was no way I was going to start my first project by saying "I don't know."

I buried myself into a spreadsheet with client data. A few twenty-hour work days later, I still had not figured it out. My deadline was fast approaching, and I did not see a good ending. I started thinking about the snowball effect. If I failed at my first project, that means I would fail at this job, which means my career would never get off the launchpad, which means I wouldn't be able to pay off my student debts. My entire life would be ruined at age twenty-seven. I felt more stress than ever before.

Thankfully, a colleague saw how stressed I was and asked me if I needed help. We figured it out. I felt like my career had been spared. I turned in the analysis to the manager and got a real night of sleep for the first time in days.

I look back now at that story, and my stress at the time seems so out of perspective. The analysis never even got presented to the client. It was correct, but just not important. I don't even remember the name of the client.

By my tenth day on the Camino, I was hitting my groove. I had reached a truce with my twisted ankle by taking on walking sticks. I had survived my first infected-blister scare. I felt how grueling the next three weeks of walking would be, but I felt confident that I could do it.

As I walked out of the urban bustle of Burgos, I got my first taste of the *meseta*, the large expanse of flat, treeless terrain in the middle of Spain. There was little to see between Burgos and the next stop for the night in my itinerary, a town called Hontanas. At about nineteen miles, this stage was above the fifteen-mile average on my plan, but at least it was flat. Since the terrain was also treeless, I could see for miles. After several hours, I started to worry, as I didn't see any sign of Hontanas. I checked and rechecked the maps, but felt like I was on the path, so I kept going. About twenty minutes later, Hontanas thankfully, and magically, appeared when I got to a ridge and saw it nestled down in a valley. It had been a long day. I had a big smile on my face as I walked into town to the hostel. I was starving, so I decided to eat before checking in.

After taking off my pack and sipping on my celebratory beer at the end of the day, I pulled out my itinerary to get my reservation confirmation code for check-in. It took me a minute to see my mistake. I did have the name Hontanas as my destination on my itinerary listed that day, but my hotel was in Castrojeriz, another six miles away.

I couldn't believe I had made such a mistake. I had checked my travel planning many times. But sometimes I couldn't find a place to stay with a website in the town I wanted, so I looked for the next closest thing on the map. That must have been the case here. I thought about my options. If I listened to my aching feet and back, I would just throw my itinerary out and stay here. But then I realized that would be like the first domino and could negate all the following nights of my plan and all my reservations.

I was deflated as I put my backpack on and walked out. The whole Camino had been a challenge, but this was going to be one that wasn't going to be fun. My screw-up meant I had jammed two days of walking into one day. Thankfully I had enough daylight left to do it, but I was not looking forward to it. This was one challenge I was not welcoming.

After the Camino, I look back on that as a great day. Even though it was one of the most grueling and least entertaining days on the Camino, it was a day on the Camino. The worst day doing something I love is better than the best day doing something I dread.

CAMINO LEADERSHIP LESSON—
PUT CHALLENGES INTO PERSPECTIVE.

▶ *Appreciate Your Job:* When you have a bad day or more at work, you may be tempted to say you don't like your job. Before you do that, think about how you would feel if you didn't have your job. Think about how excited you were when you got the job. Your worst day on the job is probably better than a good day without the job. Remind yourself before you complain. Remind the people you lead as well.

▶ *Put Mistakes into Perspective:* When a mistake happens at work, it is important to put it into perspective before reacting. Unless you work in certain fields, the mistakes you or others make don't mean there is going to be a loss of life or limb. While mistakes may not be possible to undo, they probably just mean a loss of time, money, or pride. You can deflate stress and tension by putting things into perspective before taking corrective measures.

CHAPTER 4

Make Others
Feel Welcome

Statue of a pilgrim resting on the Camino.

KIND PEOPLE ON AND AROUND THE CAMINO MAKE PILGRIMS FEEL welcome. I remember an old man passing out candy to pilgrims with a big smile and his own stamp to add to pilgrims' collections. I also remember taking a picture of a house with "Buen Camino" painted in huge letters on its driveway. These were just two of many examples of locals making me feel welcome. Rosie from Australia felt welcomed in a more direct way: "One day we were walking in the pouring rain, in a very small town. A woman saw us and came outside and, in her limited English, offered for us to go inside her house until the rain had stopped. Such a generous welcome for someone so cold, wet, and tired! I am often reminded of this moment and try to make others feel welcome as selflessly as this woman did us."

At first glance, I thought this "Make Others Feel Welcome" value was such common sense that it was a waste of space on the list of values a pilgrim should follow. I learned to greet people with a "hello" as a child. When a relative came over, I was taught to welcome them with a hug. Somewhere along the way to adulthood, though, I forgot about the importance of making others feel welcome in the workplace. As a "let's get down to business" person at work, I thought the best way to make others feel welcome was to show that I was well prepared for our meeting. Preparation showed that I respected them and their time. I viewed lengthy "small talk" at the beginning of meetings as phony and wasteful. The Camino taught me that talk is never small if it helps people feel welcome.

Greet People in a Meaningful Way

The Camino provides intensive training in how to greet people in a meaningful way. A pilgrim meets new people every day on the trail, in the pilgrim hostels (*albergues* in Spanish), or at meals. These interactions are often in a second language with a person from a different culture. They are a powerful way to learn to greet people in a meaningful way.

Some of the Camino lessons are tactical. Rosie from Australia shared the lesson she'd gotten from her Camino: "I take more time out now to stop and talk to people, actually listen to them and what is going on in their lives, rather than the perfunctory hello, how are you, good-bye." Jodi, a pilgrim from the USA, shared her Camino lesson: "I am trying to change how I greet people walking past me. Most of the time, people say 'How are you' but don't really want to know. I am going to say 'good to see you' instead, unless I have the time to hear how they are doing."

Some of the lessons come from being on the receiving end of a best practice in welcoming. Jackie, a community relations manager from the USA, shared her story: "I met a lady on the first day who did not speak English. She noticed that I had struggled up one of the climbs, and she asked me (in her native language, which I couldn't understand) if I was okay. I knew that's what she was asking, because she used her hands to describe it. I nodded that I was okay, and she smiled. I saw her every day for five days and she asked me the same question, but each day she said it more like a statement. So not like 'Are you okay?' but rather, 'YOU are okay!' And she'd smile at me and do a thumbs-up. She was so welcoming with that, and I came home wanting to be more like that."

Sometimes a simple smile can be all it takes to make others feel welcome. Sandy, a mother from the USA, "was on a train from Santiago to Madrid after my Camino, and a non-English-speaking old woman sat next to me on the train. We communicated with smiles and gestures. I bought her a soda, she gave me hard candies. It was a magical seven hours, and when I left, we hugged. Never a word spoken. . . . A smile communicates a lot, even if you don't speak the language."

As an executive before the Camino, I chaired a lot of meetings and took that role seriously because they consumed a lot of a precious, nonrenewable resource: time. More than once, I calculated the cost of a meeting by taking the average per-hour salary times the number of people in the room. Some big meetings represented an investment approaching $5,000 based on that calculation. If I were asked to approve a request for $5,000 for equipment, I would want to know if it was an efficient use of money. I prided myself on running meetings efficiently. We started and ended on time. We ensured that all the logistics were set. We got through everything on the agenda. We recorded the "action items" coming out of each meeting and tracked their completion in the next sessions. We even scored each meeting based on our success in completing all the above tasks. In short, we ran our meetings like finely tuned machines.

Somewhere along the way, I'd lost sight of the human part of the meetings I chaired. While those meetings were routine for me, they were not for everyone else in the room. For junior staff, these meetings were often a rare chance for them to personally interact with me or other executives. They may have been working a long time on the material being covered in the meeting. By skipping the "small talk" to begin the meeting, I wasn't just saving time: I wasn't investing in making others feel welcome.

The Camino has cracked the code on making others feel welcome through the greeting every *peregrino* lives by—"Buen Camino!" Translated literally from Spanish, "Buen Camino!"

means "Good Way!" or "Good Walk!" Like every new *peregrino*, I quickly embraced the "Buen Camino!" greeting on the trail. I thought it made me seem cool, identifying me as a pilgrim. It took me a while to understand it beyond the superficial meaning, however. When said from one pilgrim to another, it is shorthand for, "Hello. I recognize and share the mission you are on, and I wish you success." When said from a local person to a *peregrino*, it is shorthand for, "Hello. You are welcome here. I understand the mission you are on, and I wish you success." In just two words, people greet each other with sincere empathy and support.

CAMINO LEADERSHIP LESSON—
GREET PEOPLE IN A MEANINGFUL WAY.

▸ *Remember Names*—The first key to greeting others in a meaningful way is to acknowledge them by name if you can. As you get further up the organizational chart, you have more names to remember and it gets more difficult. The payoff is worth it, however. I was impressed early in my career by an executive several layers above me. He had hundreds of people in his organization, so I challenged him to remember my name in a moment of immature bravado. When he smiled and called me by name, I was impressed. I felt like he "knew me." Whatever he did to remember hundreds of names, it obviously was meaningful to me since I remember it twenty-five years later. Who will remember you for remembering them in twenty-five years?

▸ *Show Interest*—Recall something else about a person you meet, such as a project or experience. In large organizations, keeping up with individuals can take effort. There is a payoff. A worker far down an organizational chart might feel like her hard work is invisible to top executives. A sign of notice from the top executive can mean a lot to her.

▸ *Show Empathy*—What you say to greet a person is only half the battle. Reacting to his response is the other half. Listen to what he says. Read how he says it. If you sense that he is stressed, acknowledge that you appreciate that fact. A simple "hang in there" can say much sometimes.

Be the Kind Stranger

Many pilgrims have an experience with a stranger who performs a random act of kindness on the Camino. Sometimes these kind strangers are people who live in a village along the Camino. Sometimes they are fellow pilgrims. Terry, a pilgrim from England, shared this story: "I am fifty-nine and, five years ago, I wouldn't even walk to the shops. After seeing the film *The Way*, I said to myself that I would do it. Many laughed at my intentions, and I was stirred on to do it. As I walked up the Pyrenees to the first *albergue* at Roncesvalles by myself, it started to rain. The adrenaline from the day before had left me, and I was not in a good place. I started to doubt myself and to think, 'Why have I done this?' From out of the mists came a Japanese woman who just nodded to me and handed me a chocolate bar. She disappeared, but the snack fortified me and I got to the top."

I would like to think that someone considers me a "kind stranger" for some good deed I've done in my career. But I can't think of any. The tough part about the "stranger" part is, even if I was, they probably couldn't figure out how to connect with me afterward to tell me.

I did get a chance to see someone on my team realize the payback of being a "kind stranger." The elections in 2008 saw a record turnout of voters in Washington, DC, seeking to vote via absentee ballot. The local board of elections was overwhelmed. Complaints started pouring in to the mayor's office, where I was working at the time. The board of elections, which was independent of the mayor's office, called us for emergency assistance. Luckily, the mayor was not on the ballot that year. I led a relief effort, and, thanks to the help of dozens of volunteers, everyone who got their absentee ballot request in on time was able to vote.

After that effort, one of the volunteers, Matt, shared a story with me. He was covering the phones when an elderly woman called to say she hadn't received her ballot in the mail. It was now just hours before her deadline to mail it back. She wasn't physically able to travel to the office to pick it up. She was distraught. She had never thought she would get a chance to vote for an African-American president. Now she saw that chance slipping away. Matt checked with one of the election staff and then offered to deliver her ballot personally. He paid for a cab to get to her home in a neighborhood he had never before been to. When the woman answered the door and saw Matt, she cried. She told him that, early in her life, if she had seen someone who looked like Matt on election day, she expected to be hassled, not helped. She was so happy, she wanted to give him something as a thank-you. She grabbed a can of ginger ale and insisted that he take it. Months later, I saw that unopened can of ginger ale still on Matt's desk. Wherever he is, I hope it still serves as a reminder of the power of being a kind stranger.

My Camino was saved by a kind stranger. My first bad blister appeared on a Sunday night in a small town. Other pilgrims told me the local pharmacy was open until 9 or 10 P.M., so I hurried there, one limp at a time. When I got to the door, it was locked with a "closed" sign in Spanish. I didn't knock, but an older gentleman was in there cleaning and came to the door. He

opened it and simply asked me if I was a *peregrino*. I said "sí"
and showed him my blister as a shortcut to a word they didn't
teach in my high school Spanish class. He let me in and, without another word, he pushed a button and said something on
the call box outside the door. A few minutes later, an irritated
pharmacist appeared from outside and asked me what prescrip-
tion I needed. I pointed to my blister. She huffed and, while giving me the antiseptic gel, she angrily told the cleaning man that
this wasn't what she considered an "emergency" for her after-
hours on-call status. The old man played dumb with a "sorry, I
misunderstood the American" shrug. I paid, and he showed me
to the door. Letting me out, he took my hand with a conspirato-
rial smile and a wink and said, "Buen Camino."

CAMINO LEADERSHIP LESSON—
BE THE KIND STRANGER.

▸ *Have an Open Door Policy*—Show that you are willing to
help people by being easily accessible. Keep your office door
open. Walk around. Schedule open office hours. Find your
own style for showing people that you are accessible.

▸ *Plan for Strangers in Need*—If you have an "open door" to
the public, be prepared to handle strangers in need, especially during times outside normal business hours. Develop a
protocol and train your employees on it.

▸ *Celebrate the Stories*—I was working late at the office one
night when my desk phone rang. When I picked it up, I was
surprised to find that the number to our customer complaints center had rolled over to my phone. The caller had a
pressing problem. I listened and dutifully wrote down the
particulars of his complaint. I never mentioned to the gentleman that he was talking to the COO and not a CSR (cus-

tomer service representative) or that our open hours were long past. Once I had all the information, I walked my handwritten note down to the desk of the leader of the call center, who was one of my direct reports. By carefully handling the call myself, I wanted to show the call center staff how importantly I viewed every call that came in to them.

Welcome Help

Many pilgrims need help at some point during the Camino. The Camino teaches pilgrims to welcome help. Some pilgrims need help to start the Camino. Jodi, from the USA, shared her story: "My friend walked the Camino with me because I dared to ask if she would. Not a normal thing for me to initiate. I have been so blessed because of that question and how it has changed both of our lives." Some people need help to complete the Camino. Carol, a retired furniture-store manager from the USA, shared her Camino story: "The Camino taught me to let others help me. I'm fairly stubborn and a giver, not a taker, so it's hard even now to accept help. However, on the Camino, I was very grateful. And since I was a woman walking alone, many people helped me. I was not feeling well when I arrived at Montes de Oca. I found a bunk in the schoolhouse. I was alone. It was damp and cold. I ventured out, it was a Sunday, late, and only found a Coke and small bag of chips at a bar to bring back to eat. In the morning I put on my plastic rain poncho (it was pouring rain). The Camino was either through the woods or up a hill toward Burgos. I was still not feeling well, so I stuck out my thumb to hitch a ride. A lovely young man in a delivery truck picked me up. I was so cold, he gave me his work gloves (a hole in a few fingers) and made me keep them. He was so, so kind. He drove me to the top of the hill and wished me a buen Camino. His kindness gave me the strength to keep going."

Before the Camino, I'd prided myself on my ability to analyze my way through any problem at work. I loved showing off my creativity in finding data and my sophistication in analyzing it. I didn't want to ask others for help. I felt guilty about putting a burden on others. I also secretly worried about sharing credit.

A couple of jobs before my Camino, when I was working for the mayor of DC, the first inauguration of President Obama happened on our watch. The mayor is responsible for making sure the city is ready to host the crowds attending the ceremony and parade. With an attendance of 1.8 million people, President Obama's inauguration attracted the largest recorded crowd in DC history. My role helping prepare for the inauguration taught me how shortsighted my attitude toward requesting help was. We heard rumors that thousands of charter buses were going to bring people to the inauguration. If true, they would be turned away because the downtown area would be cordoned off in a security zone. That would mean tens of thousands of Americans who had traveled many hours on a bus to witness history would have been stuck in a massive bus traffic jam. Instead of hoisting their children on their shoulders on the Mall to watch history, people coming to attend would be stuck in traffic, without even a television. We were not going to let that happen.

I was tasked to assess the rumors and make a plan. I impressed myself with the data I was able to find. I tracked down historical estimates of the number of buses DC had handled before and how many buses there were in the US. I summed up by telling Dan, the deputy mayor, that I didn't know how many buses were planning to come, but that it indeed could be a problem.

Then Dan smiled and said, "Why don't you just ask them? Somebody in the federal government must regulate charter buses. Find out who and ask them to send you an email list." That hadn't occurred to me. Why would a federal agency help a stranger from a city government?

When we called the federal agency and described our problem, they immediately agreed to help. They quickly sent us the email address for every bus charter company in the country. We emailed all the bus companies to verify if thousands were coming. They were. We developed a radical plan to deploy the National Guard to close hundreds of blocks of downtown streets to turn them into temporary bus parking lots within walking distance of the event. After we finalized the plan, we emailed instructions to the bus companies. They complied. Every bus got parked and every passenger got back on their correct bus on Inauguration Day. Crisis averted.

On the Camino, I walked through many small, sleepy country villages along the trail. I stopped for lunch in a café in one quiet town and sat by a window while I ate a sandwich. The only sign of life outside was three older men sitting in plastic chairs in the shade in front of a house. They didn't seem to be talking or doing much, other than just sitting next to each other watching pilgrims go by. I supposed it was a better pastime than being inside watching television alone.

A couple of other pilgrims who had just finished eating left the café. They looked around for a yellow arrow and, when they didn't see any, decided to go to the left. Instantly, the three men sitting in the shade started yelling and pointing to get the pilgrims' attention. They were pointing them in the other direction to show them the correct way to continue on the Camino. The pilgrims stopped, said thank you, and turned to follow the men's directions. The old men waved them on and bid them farewell with a "Buen Camino."

The speed of their reactions made me think that these three men did this regularly. Then it dawned on me that these men weren't just people-watching; they were waiting for these opportunities to redirect lost pilgrims. They were perfectly positioned across the street from the only café in town. The corner they were on would have been an ideal place for a painted yellow arrow, as corners like that usually had. The suspicious part of me wondered if these guys were sitting in front of the arrow to obscure it so their help would be needed.

I finished my sandwich a few minutes later. As I walked out, I, too, looked for an arrow, and when I didn't see one, I purposely went the wrong way. Once again, the old men leaped into action and pointed me in the other direction. I thanked them and they "Buen Camino"-ed me. I smiled as I wondered how many times they had done this ritual before.

As I walked on, that interaction made me think about how I offered and received help in my career. I loved giving advice. If someone sought my advice, I took it as a sign of respect. It gave my ego a boost. It made me feel helpful.

On the flip side, however, I realized I didn't ask others for advice very often. If I didn't know something, I would rather figure it out myself. I didn't want to show weakness. I didn't want to bother other people. And if people gave me unsolicited advice, I would often be defensive and take it as criticism. Far from welcoming help from others, I pushed it away.

A light bulb went off that told me I should be more welcoming of help from others. Not only would I benefit from any assistance I received, I would also be building a stronger relationship with the person helping me. The person helping me would be investing in my success. That would help me get her support in the future. I would be giving her the same ego boost and sense of value I got. Simply by enabling others to grant the gift of help, I would also be giving a gift.

CAMINO LEADERSHIP LESSON—
WELCOME HELP.

▶ *Identify Helpers*—Identify people who can help you. Identify the incentive those people have to help you. Figure out how to appeal to them. In some cases, all you can appeal to is their spirit of generosity. Often you can find some other incentive for them. In my charter bus story, for example, the deputy mayor sensed that the federal agency would be keen to get involved with the inauguration. It was a small agency and would be eager to take advantage of a rare opportunity to get the attention of the incoming administration.

▶ *Solicit Help*—Weak leaders fear help. They worry that accepting help will be seen as a sign that they are not up to their job. They see offers of help from others as a vote of no-confidence. Don't be a weak leader. Be open to offers of help. Encourage them. Ask for good ideas from all parts of your organization. Help will make you better at your job. More importantly, you will also be modeling that behavior to others.

▶ *Require Openness to Help*—Let your team members know that you expect them to be open to receiving help from others. Make it explicit in their goals and expected competencies.

▶ *Acknowledge Help*—Soliciting offers of help is great; but if you don't act on those offers you receive, you will end up looking phony. Thank people who offer help and give feedback if the help turns out to be useful.

CHAPTER 5

Live in the Moment

The author on the Camino.

A PILGRIM EXPERIENCES SO MANY MOMENTS ON THE CAMINO, HE IS overwhelmed by the volume and forced to "live in the moment." Deb, a pilgrim from Australia, captured it this way: "To walk is to see and hear what is not possible in a car. To hear the quiet, to feel the rough pilgrim-walked ground under your boots, to taste the sweat on your lips. . . . We take for granted what we have, we are all too busy to look up at the sky, at the shape of the clouds. To stop and feel the wind on your face or the warmth of the sun on your skin. To walk in the forest alone, to hear the birds and the water trickling in the stream and to feel a bit cooler in the shade of the trees. Walking alone, you notice these things."

I was skeptical of the "Live in the Moment" value when I first read it. I thought it sounded trite and superficial—something I expected more on a bumper sticker than on my Camino passport. While I had prepared to coexist with the religious aspects of the Camino, I paused and thought I'd underestimated its "new age hippie-ness." It didn't take me long to realize the power this simple phrase represented and how it could help me as a leader if I found ways to apply it.

Remove Weapons of Mass Distraction

The Camino forces many pilgrims to reduce their use of mobile electronic devices. I don't recall hearing a single mobile phone ring on another pilgrim during my month on the Camino. Some pilgrims turn off mobile phones to avoid roaming fees. Some turn them off to avoid distractions. Roberta, a retired government executive from Canada, used her Camino as a teaching moment. "The walk with my grandchildren was particularly important because they had to leave their tablets and iPhones at home and embrace the journey. They learned that even when it is difficult, you have to carry on; because if you stop in the middle of the road there is no food, no place to sleep, and no one to do it for you."

Before my Camino, I'd always had my phone at the ready at work. In fact, I had two of them strapped to my belt—one for work and one for personal use. I looked like a nerdy Batman. In most meetings, I put them on the table in front of me so I could see if I had a new message. I was trained to immediately check the slightest beep or buzz. I felt like I was so important, I had to be reachable at all times. I was important, so somebody important might be trying to reach me, after all.

My phone addiction was not unique. If I looked around the room in any large meeting, at least a few people were paying more attention to their phones than the meeting.

I also liked using my phone and earphones to tune out people outside the office. Sometimes, after a day full of meetings, I just wanted a rest from conversation. Even though I was usually listening to audiobooks or podcasts on a low volume so I could hear others, those white ear buds were shields I hid behind.

I planned my phone addiction into my Camino. Since the Camino was going to be my first monthlong hike, I worried about getting bored along the way. I did the math and figured that if I was going to be on the trail about eight hours a day for about thirty days, that meant I had 240 hours I would need to fill to entertain myself during the walk. I love listening to audiobooks while I bike or run, so I loaded up my phone with a bunch of books—the longer the better. I was excited about getting two things done at once—hiking the Camino while getting through my reading list.

My first day walking the Camino, I had my phone at the ready but decided to hold off for a while until I got bored. In the end, I never put those earphones in on my whole Camino.

Keeping those shields in my pocket changed my Camino. It was easy to strike up conversations with other pilgrims along the trail. I had a common bond with other pilgrims that provided easy conversational icebreakers. "Where did you start today?" or, "Where are you staying tonight?" I met dozens of my fellow pilgrims on the trail from simple exchanges like that. Many of those introductions have blossomed into lasting friendships. In the years since my hike, I have made trips to several European countries to visit my Camino friends. Those relationships, one in particular, have changed my life for the better.

When I think about what my Camino would have been like if I'd had those earphones in, I shudder. If even one of those initial interactions hadn't happened because I looked closed-off to meeting new people, it is not an exaggeration to say that my life would be worse off.

CAMINO LEADERSHIP LESSON—
REMOVE WEAPONS OF MASS DISTRACTION.

▶ *Be Self-Aware*—When you check your phone during a meeting or conversation, you are sending out a rude message: "I don't even know who is trying to get my attention, but I know paying attention to them is more important than paying attention to you."

▶ *Set a "No Distractions" Policy*—Be the champion of a strict "no electronics usage" policy in meetings. If an attendee needs to use his mobile device, he should excuse himself from the meeting. Clearly set this expectation in all meetings you run.

▸ *Enforce the Policy*—Setting a policy and not enforcing it is worse than having no policy at all. Figure out ways you can enforce the policy consistently. Consider preventative measures, such as making attendees give up their phones before starting the meeting. Consider enforcement measures, such as calling out rule-breakers in an acceptable way. You could do it bluntly—e.g., "Please do that business outside and come back to this meeting when you are available." Maybe you can do it in a more lighthearted way that still makes the point. You can do it less obviously, too, by targeting your questions in the meeting to people distracted by their phone.

▸ *Model the Policy*—Lead by example. Hold yourself to the "no mobile distractions" rule in all meetings you attend, not just the ones you run. People will notice.

▸ *Champion the Policy*—Once your policy is working consistently, help your larger organization adopt the same policy. Advocate its effectiveness. Gather "before versus after" facts or comments to help make the case. Invite outsiders to sit in on your meetings to observe the positive impact of the policy. Write about the experience.

Look Up from the Plan and Experience the Journey

The Camino teaches pilgrims to look up and experience the journey instead of simply focusing on reaching the end in Santiago de Compostela. Pilgrims walk through hundreds of miles of scenery and dozens of villages. They experience many pleasures and pains along the way. After a while, the Camino over-whelms a pilgrim in a good way.

Pam, a pilgrim from the USA, explained it this way: "The Camino taught me to accept the challenges in front of me in the moment and each day. It taught me that although life can sometimes be challenging and painful, we must not forget to 'look up' and recognize the beauty around us. When I walked the Camino, it was an extremely hot summer in northern Spain, my feet were blistered, and the hills and mountains sometimes seemed like a daunting task; and then I would look up and think, 'Wow, look at the beauty that surrounds me.' That's the lesson . . . if we focus on the pain of the challenge or worry about what's to come and fail to recognize the beauty and love around us, we miss the point of life."

Two Caminos taught this lesson to Valerie, a public-relations specialist from Canada: "Both times, it taught me to slow down and truly see/experience things around me rather than racing through the day, week, life! It also taught me to be open to the lessons the Camino was teaching me: patience; things don't al-ways go as planned; not everyone experiences the Camino the same way or learns the same lessons even though walking the same route side by side—much as in life :-)."

Pearl, from New Zealand, learned to focus on the experience instead of sticking to her plans: "A couple of weeks in, I had been walking on a knee injury that was getting worse each day. . . . This particular day, my daughter had told me we were NOT walking today, we had to bus to the next town. I finally relented to the decision, and we stayed under our sleeping bags as every-one else click-clacked out the door that morning. I was really upset, as my plan was to walk the whole way. I struggled up-stairs for breakfast, and we sat in a corner. As I was at the table getting tea, with tears streaming down, a tall Italian cyclist came up and gave me a huge hug, pointed to his plastered knee—'Problemo'—held up several fingers indicating (I assumed) how many days he had taken off, then said, 'Okay, it's okay.' He enveloped me in a hug once more and left. That of course made me cry more, but less out of self-pity. From then on, when something happened we didn't expect, we said: 'It's okay.' Now, back home, I don't let the small things bother me anymore; I just keep telling myself it is okay that today's path has taken a different turn and we will see where it leads. I am much more relaxed about a lot of things now, not letting the small stuff get to me and seeing that my journey in life can change unexpectedly, but that's okay too. . . . Take every opportunity that arises—and work out how afterwards!"

My experience in the Washington, DC, mayor's office during the first Obama inauguration also taught me to look up from the plan and experience the journey. It took an enormous amount of planning and work by people across the entire DC government to make sure that day went smoothly for the historically large crowd of attendees. I spent a lot of time in the center of that, helping coordinate and keep the mayor informed about the preparations. For the forty-eight hours around the inauguration, I was in the city's emergency command center, running around to check if the plan was working. That is, until I got "shushed." It took a lot of guts for that person to "shush" the guy from the mayor's office, but I soon realized that he was right. I took my eyes off the communication traffic coming in from the field and looked up at the television. Aretha Franklin was singing at the inauguration ceremony. All the eyes in the emergency center were glued to the television, many with tears. That moment put the historic nature of the ceremony into view. Yes, we had a plan to stick to, but we had to remember to look up and experience it as humans, too. I felt embarrassed.

On most hiking and biking trails, I frequently look at my map. Most trails I have done have been waymarked, ranging from an occasional signpost to a simple stripe of paint on a tree. From bad experiences getting lost on other trails, I learned I couldn't simply rely on seeing waymarks. Some might be missing. Some I might miss. Checking my map frequently had become second nature to me on hikes and bikes.

Then I met the Camino, the easiest-to-follow trail I had ever experienced. It was very well marked, with formal signposts complemented by many simple, yellow-painted arrows. Beyond following the markers, I also was able to follow the path by feel and common sense. In towns, I figured out the path typically followed the main shopping route. When I wasn't sure which way to go, I would look up to see if I could see any pilgrims ahead of me.

When I figured out I didn't need to keep my nose in my guidebook's maps, my experience changed. I ended up following exactly the same route I had planned, without needing to pull out my plans all the time. The few times I did veer off my plan were intentional because I decided to go with the flow of my fellow *peregrinos* instead of sticking to my own plan.

By keeping my eyes up and away from my plans on paper, I experienced much more than I would have. I just focused on reaching my planned destination each day and followed the flow and markings to get there. I knew that as long as I met my one simple goal for each day, I would hit my larger goal of completing the path and catching my plane back home. That focus was liberating. I often look at my pictures from my Camino. Feeding a donkey. Watching a shepherd lead a train of hundreds of sheep. Seeing a nun jamming on a guitar. I wonder how many of those pictures I would have missed if I had been looking down at paper instead of out at the world.

CAMINO LEADERSHIP LESSON—
LOOK UP FROM THE PLAN AND EXPERIENCE THE JOURNEY.

▸ *Plan for Experiences*—If you have a project plan, identify points where you should insert more time to experience the happenings around your project. These could be holidays or other important events in your organization. They could be key checkpoints in the project that would be natural points for celebration or reflection. Build these into your project plans so you don't miss them.

▸ *Build in Slack*—Some meaningful experiences will not be predictable. A piece of surprise good news could emerge. An unexpected challenge could be overcome. Whatever they are, you should build buffer time into your project plans to enable unplanned breaks without risking your project's due date.

▸ *Create Outlets for Experience Sharing*—Deliverables, gateways, risks, and other parts of a project plan are natural things around which to organize team meetings. Organizing your meetings only around those can stifle experience sharing. Add an item to your meeting agendas where people can share the lessons learned and other experiences.

Control Your Calendar

A typical pilgrim has set start and end dates for his Camino, but not a rigid schedule within each day. Many pilgrims find that break, from the patterns they're used to back at work, to be liberating. Kat, a mortgage broker from the USA, explained it this way: "I have a very stressful and intense job—I don't know where my days go, but I spend an average of sixteen hours/day working. On the Camino, it was thrilling to get up and know the ONLY thing I needed to concern myself with was getting from Point A to Point B." For Steve, a software developer from Ireland, "The Camino was all about getting back to basic living. Getting up at dawn, setting off for the day, finding a little café for a carb-filled breakfast. Then on to the destination for the day, check into the *albergue*, take a siesta, get an evening meal, and then to bed. Doing the same thing day after day. Those days were so simple and nice, a far cry from now being a dad to three small children."

My calendar at work was out of control before I did my Camino. Since about a fourth of the entire agency worked in the department I headed, I was asked to attend many meetings to represent my team. Every night before I left, my assistant would give me a printout of my calendar for the next day. It would show a day full of meetings, sometimes with two or three booked at the same time. Since meetings were back-to-back, I would often be late for the start of one when the previous one went long. My days seemed like a combination of musical chairs and a scavenger hunt. I would get up from one chair after an hour or so and then have to find the room with the next chair I would sit in for the next meeting.

In addition to the calendar printout, there was always a folder underneath with a thick stack of papers. These were the materials that would be covered in each meeting. Not only was every minute of my workday preprogrammed; I also had homework each night to read through to prepare for each meeting.

My calendar had become my boss; in fact, it was the most micromanaging boss I'd ever had. If I'd had a human boss who told me what I would be doing with every minute of my time, I would have found a new job and boss. Yet this was what I had done.

Each day on the Camino was full of activity, but it wasn't

scheduled minute by minute. I knew my ultimate goal (Santiago de Compostela), and I had a target each day that would ensure that I made my goal. But I didn't program each day in thirty-minute increments. I started the day with the sun. I stopped for a rest or a meal when the need and opportunity arose, not when hands on a clock told me I had to. By freeing me from a detailed daily calendar, I was able to more fully experience my journey that day. If I met someone interesting at lunch and wanted to linger, I could do so. If I enjoyed a scenic vista, I could take the time to break out my camera and take plenty of pictures. I was in control of my time.

Time is the most fixed and scarce resource that leaders have. A leader needs to be as smart in investing her time as she is with any other resource. If she becomes a slave to her calendar, she needs to take control by firing her current calendar and starting over.

Beyond managing his own time better, a leader should realize he sets the tone for his whole team. Any improvements he makes in managing his calendar can become a model for others.

CAMINO LEADERSHIP LESSON—
CONTROL YOUR CALENDAR.

▸ *Identify Your "Must-Attend" Meetings*—These are the meetings you, and only you, must attend. These meetings include your one-on-one meetings with your boss and your direct reports. They would also include meetings where, by virtue of your job title, you hold the authority to make decisions required in those meetings. Identify ways to make these meetings more efficient uses of time. Consider shorter meeting times or reduced frequency. See if a "drop-by" or returned phone call could suffice.

▸ *Manage Your "Must-Be-Represented" Meetings*—These are the meetings you are invited to so you can represent your organization's interests in an indirect (e.g., non-voting or approval-granting) way. Identify the few most important meetings in which you want to stay closely involved. Keep your attendance in those. For the other meetings, identify the best people on your team to represent you. Seek to distribute and rotate the delegation assignments. Most delegates will appreciate the increased exposure. Set the expectation with each delegate of how they are to represent you. Clarify what they are empowered to do and how they are to keep you informed.

▸ *Manage Your "Other" Meetings*—These are meetings that made it onto your calendar but are not "musts" for you. Identify which of these are inefficient uses of your time. Decide how to screen those in the future.

▸ *Reinvest Your Free Time*—Use the time you free up wisely. Visit people you don't often see in meetings. Build relationships with other stakeholders. Make it dedicated "thinking" time. Don't let it get soaked up again by new meetings.

▸ *Redo Your Calendar and Test*—Reset your calendar and implement it over a test phase. Make it clear that you may take back the meetings you delegate as you see how it works. Review your calendar periodically and readjust as necessary.

CHAPTER 6

Share

Free wine fountain at Bodegas Irache.

THE CAMINO TEACHES THE VALUE OF SHARING TO PILGRIMS. Pilgrims' possessions are limited to what they can carry in a backpack. Perhaps because material possessions are so few, they seem less important. Sharing becomes a reaction and a habit.

Jo Anne, a pilgrim from the USA, learned a powerful lesson about sharing on her Camino: "For months before leaving for the Camino, I had a dream that I met a man on the Camino who had hurt his knee, so I gave him my hiking pole. I don't hike with hiking poles because I have a bad arm, but I took two with me just because of my dream. On the Camino, I met two men, one of whom had hurt his knee. He asked if I knew where he could buy a hiking pole. I told him about my dream and that he could have my pole. The man burst into tears and excused himself. His friend, who had been in buying coffee, came out and asked me what had happened. I said I had given the man my hiking pole. The friend then told me that the gentleman that I'd given my pole to had lost his wife a few months before and had never cried. Then he thanked me for helping his friend to finally grieve for his wife. I ran into them again a few days later, and the gentleman I'd given my pole to told me he felt like a huge weight had been lifted off his shoulders. I'm glad that I lugged those poles around for a few hundred miles: I learned such a wonderful lesson about sharing."

Kat, from the USA, had another example of the power of sharing: "On my first Camino, I met a guy who was trying to cope with the death of his brother. It took a lot of sacrifice for him to even GET to the Camino—financially and being away from his wife and child. He was down to his last couple of dollars. . . . I was leaving the next day. I, literally, gave him the shirt off my back—my 'lucky' supremely comfy T-shirt (donated by my dad :) and every Euro I had in my pocket. I didn't think twice about it; he would have done the same for anyone else. He was very grateful and humble but, mostly, he was an incredibly nice person who shared his stories and thoughts with me. Someone I will always remember as one of my favorite people I met on my journey."

When I read this value of Sharing for the first time, it seemed fitting for the spirit of the Camino, but I wondered how relevant it would be for life after the Camino. Earning an MBA in finance taught me more about the art of negotiating than the joy of sharing. I looked at life in the business world as a zero-sum game: I had to get more than the other person to win. I was ready to put that mind-set aside for my month on the Camino and go with the flow and share. I didn't have that much to share anyway, as all my possessions fit in a backpack for the month. As I expected, sharing was a natural act on the Camino. What I didn't expect was that I would find ways to incorporate sharing into my post-Camino business world.

Find Profitable Giveaways

Some pilgrims realize that sharing can benefit the giver as much as the receiver. The Camino taught Peter, the executive coach from the Netherlands, a valuable lesson for his business back home. "I share everything I know now. My business model has changed. You may have all my knowledge that has been published, and use it. I will suggest material if I think I can help you, or you can ask for material and I will share. Only if you want me personally to be involved, then there is an invoice involved." Lysa, a paramedic from England, summarized her Camino lesson about sharing quite elegantly: "Every time you give away something on the Camino, your backpack gets lighter."

Before my Camino, my first real leadership experience had come through student government while I was getting my MBA. I served for a year as the head of the student government that represented all the students in the university's twelve graduate and professional schools. It was a big role for me at the time, representing a population of over 10,000 students and managing a budget over $100,000. I learned many lessons in leadership in that role. One lesson only became clear after I saw it again on the Camino.

The biggest goal for our student government was to get a dedicated social space for our student population. Each of the twelve graduate and professional schools had their own student governments and spaces, but there was not a shared space where students across schools could meet. We saw that as a big un-tapped potential to help our constituents. Graduate school life can be a lonely existence, particularly for people in small pro-grams or far away from home. I still remember an engineering school student telling me how he was up all night alone in a lab watching a piece of metal bend to record when it broke. A shared social space would help students like him. As an MBA student, I also saw it as a business opportunity. All the univer-sity's graduate schools were highly rated in their field. I saw a shared space as an innovation lab, with business students mix-ing with medical and engineering students and new companies forming.

I went back to campus for my twentieth reunion and was in-vited to a reunion of graduate-student government leaders. It was held at the graduate student center, which was celebrating its thirteenth anniversary. It was bigger and busier than I had dreamed. When I was on the student government, we'd had to spend a lot of our budget on elaborate events with free food, drinks, giveaways, and entertainment to get the students out mixing together. As soon as the event ended, the students went their separate ways. We didn't see much increase in interaction across schools outside our events. When I asked what the secret was to the success of the graduate student center, the answer surprised me with its simplicity: "free coffee."

The Camino de Santiago passes through the beautiful Rioja and Navarra wine regions in the northeast of Spain. The highlight of my hike one day from Estella to Los Arcos was the wine fountain one of the wineries set up for pilgrims. At no cost, pilgrims are invited to serve themselves from the tap. The fountain is remote enough to discourage anyone but pilgrims from visiting it, and it is locked after dark. Its rules are posted on a sign with the following poem that sounds much better in Spanish than my rough English translation:

RULES OF USE

To drink without abusing
We invite you with pleasure;
To take our wine with you
We ask for some treasure.

When I reached the wine fountain, I took off my bag and decided to take a break. I filled my water bottle up with some nice red wine and relaxed and watched other pilgrims filter in as I sipped it. Many could not believe it was free. Nobody I saw abused it.

It was remarkable how much a free glass of wine lifted our spirits. It was a highlight of many conversations with other pilgrims for days afterwards. Beyond providing refreshment, the winery was giving an affirmation to pilgrims about how they appreciated the mission we were on. It was a highlight for hikers that day after some climbing. It also gave pilgrims a chance to stop and meet each other.

After I finished my wine and got back on the trail, my MBA mind started kicking in. How much was this winery spending to do this? What benefit were they getting out of it?

As I started piecing it together, I figured the cost to the winery must have been negligible. The fountain was simply attached to the wall of one of its manufacturing or distribution buildings, which meant there were not any incremental transportation costs to get it there. While it tasted great, it was probably their least expensive wine.

Then, considering the benefits to the winery, I realized that they got more than just goodwill out of it. They got great brand exposure. Many pilgrims take a picture of the fountain and share the story. The winery even has a live webcam where people can watch pilgrims drinking from the fountain, which further gets their brand (Bodegas Irache) mentioned. And some pilgrims even mention the winery in books they write about the Camino.

After my Camino, I started looking for other places where companies give away things that are of low cost to them but create big value for recipients. Professional baseball came to mind—every time a Major League baseball player tosses a ball to a young fan at the stadium. The cost of the ball is insignificant to the team, but it becomes a priceless memento once a big-league player touches it.

CAMINO LEADERSHIP LESSON—
FIND PROFITABLE GIVEAWAYS.

▸ *Identify Hidden Pockets of Value*—Many organizations are sitting on things that are of little cost or value to them but would be prized by customers or stakeholders. Some of these could be tangible, like excess production, rejects, used materials, or by-products. Some of these might be experiential, like tours of a manufacturing process or history of a product line. Assess your organization for hidden pockets of value and consider sharing them.

▸ *Identify Goals Helped by Giveaways*—If you have a goal that has been hard to achieve, consider giveaways as a new tactic. For example, if you want to create more cross-functional interactions in your organization, provide something that will attract people from all functions to gather. In one of my jobs, for example, the company provided a free foosball (table soccer) game that was a popular place for people to interact across team boundaries. Other companies provide free snacks or food to employees for that and other reasons.

▸ *Maximize Recognition*—Leaders have one valuable asset to give away that is both virtually free and limitless—recognition. It takes little effort to tell people you appreciate their work. Build channels in your organization to make recognition flow more freely. Lead by example by doing it. Make it an expectation of others you manage. Create opportunities to do it. As long as the recognition you are sharing is genuine, you can never go too far.

Share with Others

Sharing on the Camino becomes infectious. When one pilgrim shares with another, others often join in. Hans from Belgium explains: "While walking, there was a lot of sharing, especially sharing stories but also food. Everyone put a little of their own food together and the result was a feast, or so it felt like." Some pilgrims, like Larry from Australia, continue that spirit of sharing after their Camino: "After my second Camino, I found it enjoyable to help people, to listen to people, to share with people—as when we are on the Camino, that is what we do. But the Camino is a life journey, not just a simple walk—and by living and sharing with others, we enjoy our Life Camino much more."

When I moved from California to Washington, DC, several years before my Camino, I looked for volunteer opportunities as a way to get involved in the community. I saw plenty of options where I could contribute individually, such as tutoring or mentoring kids. I also wanted to meet people, so I settled on a group called Compass. Compass is an organization that recruits people with consulting experience to provide pro bono consulting to nonprofit organizations in the area. I loved that Compass organized us in teams. I joined a team that helped a nonprofit organization serving the Hispanic community. We helped them develop a new fund-raising strategy. The project was a success for the client.

The project was a big success in another way for me as well. I am still in contact with the members of that consulting team a decade later. I have worked on dozens of project teams in my for-profit consulting career, but my Compass team has had a longer-lasting camaraderie than most. We were all giving our individual time to charity, but doing it as a team. I think that created a stronger bond.

At the end of one day on the Camino, I stopped at a little store, bought some snacks and a bottle of local wine, and wandered back to my hostel. Before I got back, I noticed a couple of other pilgrims sitting in the park sharing wine and snacks. They invited me over, and we shared our food and wine. Another few pilgrims walking by joined us. Before long, we had a picnic going with strangers from several countries.

Years later, I still connect with those people on a regular basis. I've visited them in California, England, Ireland, and Sweden. I've met many people on my other travels, but none of those acquaintances turned into long-term relationships like these did. I think our ties have remained strong because we were all sharing a powerful experience together.

Those experiences taught me the power of collective sharing. When you share things as a group, it lowers barriers for others to join. It makes it more fun, too.

CAMINO LEADERSHIP LESSON—
SHARE WITH OTHERS WITH OTHERS.

▸ *Turn Team Days into Service Days*—I've worked for organizations that give teams a day off to do some fun team-building event. I've had many fun experiences on those events, from whitewater rafting, to an amusement park visit, to skiing. One of my favorite team events was building a house for the nonprofit group Habitat for Humanity. It was the best combination of fun, learning, and team-building I've ever experienced. If you are looking for a team-building event, consider charity-centered events. They can be very organized, like Habitat for Humanity. They can also be informal, like cleaning up litter from a park or beach.

▸ *Let Others Return Your Favor*—Give the people you help a

chance to return the favor. Ask if they would be willing to give you testimonials to show your organization's contribution back to the community. By sharing those testimonials, you are advertising their needs to other potential contributors.

Share Yourself

There is a saying on the Camino that after walking with someone for a mile, you know everything about them except their last name. There is something about walking across a country that makes people open up to each other. Instead of the superficial things people ask when meeting strangers in the "real world," people on the Camino share a lot of themselves. Often, people do the Camino to help deal with a loss or a big transition in their life. If pilgrims share their reasons for walking with each other, they are sharing a real piece of themselves. Hans from Belgium explained it this way: "Sharing stories and thoughts with almost-strangers that you haven't told your best friends or relatives was part relieving, knowing that it traveled further, not only inside." While relationships on the Camino are short, they are built on foundations of sharing.

As I took on bigger leadership positions in my career, I put up a wall between my work and home lives. Part of the reason was privacy. As I led teams of larger sizes, I had more people with whom I would have to share. Another reason was my respect for people's time off of work. While I enjoyed meeting colleagues' families, that usually meant doing something work-related outside normal working hours. I didn't want to ask people to cut into their personal time.

One example still sticks in my mind. One of my teams suggested several times that we get together outside of work for team-building and to meet each others' significant others. I always pushed it off with a "let's think about that," with no intention of following up and hoping it would go away. Then one of my team members took the initiative and just invited us all to a weekend dinner at her house. I RSVP'd my regrets, saying I couldn't go. I wanted to set a signal that others didn't have to feel compelled to go. I thought this would make that one go away, too. But everyone else showed up except me. I really missed the boat on that one. I overestimated how important my presence was to the team. I underestimated how important *the team* was to the team. I was being self-centered and rude.

After I left that role, I learned that some people in my organization had found it hard to connect with me. I would hear that my reputation had been as a leader driven by strategy, data, and results. I was happy to hear that. What I was not happy to hear was I also had a reputation for being distant and overly analytical. I was even told that I had sometimes come across as an "intellectual bully" who people didn't know.

I came back from my Camino much more willing to share myself. It brought me out of a shell. When a spontaneous sing-along broke out one night over dinner on the Camino, I contributed my terrible singing voice wholeheartedly. When I got back, I shared that Camino song as well with my friends at home, punishing them with my singing voice. I doubt they thought it was good, but I could tell they saw it as a good change in me. I also started to share my writing with my friends. They at least pretended to think it was good. I think they appreciated my being more communicative, anyway. Somewhere my new openness to sharing myself snowballed into this book, which I am writing for friends I have not yet met.

CAMINO LEADERSHIP LESSON—
SHARE YOURSELF.

▶ *Share Your "User's Manual"*—The longer we work with other people, the more we learn about what it is like to work with us. We all have experiences, hot buttons, styles, and viewpoints that shape the way we work with others. Sharing those with people when we start working with them can save a painful learning experience. Acknowledging your own quirks can also create an open dialogue that will help your colleagues open up with you.

▶ *Share Personal Stories*—When you are coaching others, draw upon your own experiences where helpful. If someone needs a jolt of confidence after a negative experience, share a story from your past where you overcame a similar situation. When addressing groups, use relevant personal anecdotes where appropriate to put work topics into context. If you are talking to people who are just starting at your organization, for example, tell them a story about your first day to build a connection.

▶ *Build Channels to Share Yourself*—Build ways you can connect with people at work beyond formal channels. Things like an "open door" policy or "open office hours" can be helpful. Force yourself to get out and walk around in your organization to talk with people in an informal way. Even better, carry an icebreaker, like snacks, that you can offer as a way to initiate conversations.

CHAPTER 7

Feel the Spirit of Those Who Have Come Before You

Marker for a pilgrim who died on the Camino.

PEOPLE HAVE WALKED THE CAMINO FOR OVER A THOUSAND YEARS, and today's pilgrims feel the spirit of their predecessors. Erik, from the USA, "cried when I saw the indentions on the stone stairs in the cathedrals where centuries of pilgrims had knelt before I was even born." Tiera, a human-design teacher from Hawaii, remembered "walking along a stretch of the ancient Roman Road outside of, I think, Sahagun. I could feel, almost hear, the boots of those Roman soldiers marching along." Wijnand, a social media pilgrim from the Netherlands, summed the feeling up this way: "Pilgrims of any time and any country can surely understand each other. Those who have gone before you in some way add more weight to the whole enterprise. I could sometimes almost feel them as I walked on roads that I knew have been used for almost ten centuries."

This value touched me during a trip to Germany a year after my Camino. I was visiting the village where my Prince family ancestors lived before emigrating to America in the 1700s. As one of my distant German cousins led us on a tour, I noticed the Camino scallop shell symbol in the main square. The plaque announced that it was 2,516 kilometers to Santiago. I later learned that the village was at a convergence of two paths that pilgrims from as far east as Prague used to get to Santiago. A sign next to the shell symbol said pilgrims were welcome to stay in the village's church, noting that the butcher shop had a key if the door was locked. My ancestors were baptized and married in that church in the 1600s and 1700s. I wondered if any of my ancestors had met and helped *peregrinos*. Had any been tempted to do the Camino? I had assumed that I was the first in my family to do the Camino, but now I didn't know. And that made me smile.

Honor Your Predecessors

People on the Camino today honor pilgrims from the past in different ways. My favorite story is from Tammy, a retiree from the USA:

"I had just finished a shared meal with other pilgrims at a hostel along the Camino. The hostel host asked each pilgrim to pick a piece of paper out of one of three jars—one each in English, German, and Spanish. Each piece of paper was a note that a pilgrim who had stayed in that same hostel had left for those that would follow in their footsteps. The host asked if we wanted to read our note out loud. The note I got was written in English, but I sensed English was not the writer's first language. The writer told the story of a couple who had been married for forty-five years and decided to walk the Camino together during their retirement. Before they reached Santiago de Compostela, Lola, the wife, died. The husband stopped his Camino and took his wife's remains back home for burial. Then the husband came back to Spain to pick up where he'd left off on the Camino. When he reached the end in Santiago, he, too, fell sick and died. The note closed with the writer identifying himself as the grandson of Lola and her husband, walking the Camino in their honor."

Before my Camino, I'd worked for a large bank, and when we bought a dot-com company, I was transferred to it to take a leadership role in marketing. I had a few weeks to transition, so I dug in to the data from the new team to see where I might find opportunities for improvement. I found a big one. When I started in the new role, I presented my brilliant analysis to the woman on my team in charge of that part of the program. She quickly fixed the problem. Revenue increased by 600 percent immediately in that channel. I felt like a hero. I had made an immediate, noticeable impact in my new role. I bragged about it whenever I got the chance. I figured I would get a promotion in no time.

On the first week of my Camino, I saw it as a race. I walked faster than most other pilgrims, which means I passed them at least once a day. I heard that I was starting to get a reputation for being the fast guy in the funny green hat. One group of older, slower British guys even asked me if I "was special forces military." While I modestly said no, I loved the recognition. My competitive drive had served me well in my career. I was glad people were noticing it on the Camino as well.

A few days later, the Camino almost bested me. I made a mistake in my itinerary and had to walk too far one day. I finished it, but I was humbled by the experience. The next day's hike on my Camino started with a long, grueling climb up a steep hill under an unforgiving sun. About halfway up the hill, I saw a memorial marker for a *peregrino* who had died at that spot. I needed a water break, so I stopped. I paid my respects and walked on. I would see other markers to fallen *peregrinos* on my Camino, but this one stuck in my mind. I kept thinking about this man on the marker, José G. Valiño. I only knew two things about him. Like me, he had begun walking the Camino. Unlike me (hopefully), he had not finished it.

As I walked, I wondered what had caused José's downfall. How old was he? Was he in good physical shape? Was the weather bad? How far had he walked? Then I thought about what had brought him to the Camino at all. What was his reason? What did he have to go through to even start the trail? Had he ever done anything like this before?

José helped me figure out that the Camino was not a competition. Everyone starts from different places. Everyone faces different challenges on the way. Pilgrims don't get a grade on their Compostela certificate.

I began to think about my competitive drive in my career. If I was faster than others, it didn't prove I was better. I looked back to my banking career example where I'd thought I was a hero. I realized I had no idea what it had taken to build the operation from scratch in the early dot-com space. I only saw the snapshot from when I started. Sure, I'd found one way to make the operation better, but I hadn't appreciated how hard it must have been to build the operation in the first place. I hadn't honored the people who'd built the operation I was inheriting. I didn't get that promotion.

CAMINO LEADERSHIP LESSON—
HONOR YOUR PREDECESSORS.

▸ *Lead by Example*—When you criticize your predecessors, you make yourself look bad. People will think you are looking for excuses for your own faults. When you do talk about your predecessors, use your unique perspective to understand the context around their actions.

▸ *Recognize Your Predecessors*—Create a history of your organization. Highlight the main accomplishments of your predecessors. Recognizing your history can help build your team camaraderie and identity. Look for any artifacts from your predecessors you can use as a symbol of team history.

Learn from Your Predecessors

Many pilgrims keep journals during their Camino. Some even publish them. Pilgrims have been doing this for hundreds of years. Some of these journals have survived, providing insights into how the Camino has changed, and stayed the same, over the centuries. Some of today's pilgrims read accounts from past pilgrims to inspire or prepare them to walk the Camino. Carol, from the USA, described her research: "As I was preparing for my Camino, I purchased a book called *Pilgrims' Footsteps* by Bert Slader from Northern Ireland. That book really changed my life, and I wrote Bert. We became pen pals for over ten years, and he sent me all the other books he had written. Bert passed away a year ago. We never met. Bert walked the Camino several times, and his stories were with me on my Camino."

When I do a hike or bike trip, my sense of adventure starts in the planning phase. Once I decide on a trail and dates, I dig in to the planning. Since I don't camp outside, it takes lots of research to find places to stay each night near the trail. Diving into the details of the trail gets me excited. It's like the adventure has already begun.

When I decided to hike the Camino, I eagerly dove into the planning. I've been an analyst throughout most of my career, so I love to crunch data. I found a list of all the towns and villages along the route that also listed all the mileages in between. I looked at the map and saw that Pamplona was the biggest city near the eastern border of Spain, so I decided to start there. Once I had my starting point, I knew it would be 440 miles to the end of the trail in Santiago de Compostela. After accounting for travel time, I would have twenty-nine days on the trail. I calculated that I had to walk an average of fifteen miles a day. I looked at the list of towns and saw a town called Puente de la Reina fifteen miles from Pamplona. I looked online for a hotel. Because most towns on the Camino were small, it was hard to find hotels online. I had to get creative. I found a hotel in the center of Puente de la Reina. Then I looked to see if it had a room for the night I needed. If not, I might have to reconsider my whole route. It did! I reserved it, pasted the confirmation message and number in my spreadsheet, and congratulated myself.

If I could just do this twenty-eight more times, I would not have to camp or share a room or bathroom with strangers. Through the power of my data-driven mind, I was going to be able to research my way to my own Camino. I worked long hours over the next several days to piece together an itinerary. There were many trade-off decisions to make. If I couldn't find a hotel fifteen miles from the previous one, I had to decide whether to go farther or shorter that day where there was a hotel I could reserve. That decision would have downstream consequences that would cascade through my whole itinerary. If I cut too many days short of fifteen miles, I faced at least one day with a much longer walk to make up. My head hurt working through all the permutations. But I knew my MBA-trained brain could master it. I'd learned how to calculate linear programming optimization at Wharton, after all. That had never proved useful in the real world, but it had taken a lot of effort to learn—and now I had a chance to use it. I was going to linear-program optimize the heck out of this trail.

It took me a week. I was exhausted. But at the end, I had an itinerary that was optimized. My longest segment would be nineteen miles and my shortest would be eleven miles. My itinerary was now a spreadsheet with hundreds of cells of data, ranging from distances covered to hotel addresses and emails. Thanks to all this hard work, I would have a private room and bathroom guaranteed every night. I knew I would face a lot of challenges on the Camino, but worrying about finding a room for the night would not be one. After I'd booked my last hotel reservation, I felt a huge sense of accomplishment.

As I was packing for the Camino, I wanted to find a trail map I could carry with me. I found a guidebook on Amazon and it looked great. It also looked familiar. Then Amazon reminded me I had bought the book several months earlier. It was one of the books I'd gotten when I was planning my first trail adventure of my sabbatical. Once I had decided to do the Danube River bike trail trip, I hadn't bothered to read the Camino book. Now I found the book and threw it in my backpack.

On the eve of my first day on the trail, I opened the book to look at the map. Then I realized that the maps were organized around segments of about fifteen miles per day. It also had information about the hostels along the trail. The inns in the small towns that had taken me so much work to find were in the book. I had basically re-created this itinerary. If I had just read this book, I would have saved myself a lot of work. I quit feeling so proud of my sophisticated spreadsheet itinerary.

CAMINO LEADERSHIP LESSON—
LEARN FROM YOUR PREDECESSORS.

▸ *Don't Dive In*—It can be easy to start with a new assignment by jumping right to the part that appeals to you the most. Getting into the details quickly can make you feel like you are getting off to a fast start. Instead, take a step back at the beginning of a new assignment and search for relevant history. Try to find others who have had the same or similar assignments. You can save yourself a lot of time, and embarrassment, by avoiding "reinventing the wheel."

▸ *Debrief Your Predecessors*—When you take over a leadership role, reach out to your predecessor to debrief her on the role, if possible. Get her assessment of the strengths and weaknesses of the team and the threats and opportunities facing it. Not only will you be getting useful information, you will be creating goodwill with your predecessor. By giving her a chance to share her ideas with you, she may feel invested in your success. She will likely appreciate the chance to give context around any of the actions she took.

▶ *"Read Into" New Roles*—Getting up to speed in a new leadership job is one of the best ways to ensure your success. Gather all the performance reports, studies, and other documentation you can find that can help you understand your new role. Ask your predecessor or hiring manager to help you. The time between when you are hired and when you actually start is a uniquely valuable time to prepare for your new role. You will be able to view things with a detached perspective. You won't be tainted by being responsible for past decisions. You will identify natural questions about things. Transition times are windows of opportunity to ask questions without fearing that people will judge you harshly for not knowing the answers.

▶ *Create a "Lessons Learned" Environment*—Build the infrastructure and process to ensure that your team is capturing its own "lessons learned" for future generations. Tools like a wiki-based intranet can be a great way to do this. Require your team members to close out projects by recording the lessons learned in your intranet in "after-action reports."

Get Inspiration from Your Predecessors

It is easy for Camino pilgrims to feel inspired by the Camino. For some pilgrims, the inspiration comes from feeling connected to centuries of history. Kailagh, a teacher from New Zealand, "felt a huge sense of being part of something great. . . . I felt like I was contributing to something powerful and big, a story written by time just by putting one foot in front of the other." Sandy, from the USA, "was acutely aware of the many people who had walked before me, many, many years ago. I thought of how hard it must have been for them without all our modern-day comforts." Derek, a historian from Scotland, "imagined the pilgrims who came before me—their pain and blood—in the dust and the heat. . . . And entering Santiago de Compostela—I could almost feel the pilgrims of old cheering me on and patting me on the back."

Many pilgrims say they feel a "guardian angel" watching out for them on their pilgrimage. Donal, a pilgrim from Ireland, described it this way: "Especially on the pilgrimage from Le Puy in France, there was always the feeling of the millions who had walked before. . . . As I am a slow walker, on many occasions I stepped aside to allow a pilgrim who I heard coming up behind me to pass, only to find that I was alone—the spirit of pilgrims past!"

I remember hearing and saying "the Camino will provide" at many points when problems emerged on the trail. That sense of invisible support from the past helped lower my stress during my Camino. It also made me feel inspired to live up to the high expectations set by my predecessors. Stephen, from England, captured that feeling this way: "What motivated me on the bad days was knowing that millions of people before me had walked this same route with the same pains, and they got to Santiago de Compostela."

Few workplaces can compete with the history of the Camino, but most occupations have some form of history that can be drawn upon for inspiration. Sometimes leaders have to look for it in creative places.

When I worked in the mayor's office, I appreciated the gorgeous old city hall building that housed our offices. It was an ornate granite and marble building with impractically high ceilings, grand staircases, and broad hallways that are rarely found in modern buildings. Outside, it was adorned at the top with sculptures of classical figures with robes and shields and other symbols relating to government. From my top-floor office, I could see those sculptures in a close-up way that few other observers could. From that view, I started to notice how detailed and lifelike the faces on these sculptures were. From a handlebar mustache to a cleft chin, the faces on these statues were not generic. It dawned on me that the artisans who made these sculptures must have modeled them on someone they knew. They were probably paying permanent homage to a loved one, or maybe immortalizing themselves. Whatever their motive, these artisans had left their mark on the building long past their own lifetimes. When new people started on my team at the mayor's office, I made a ritual of showing them the statues from the top-floor window and telling them the story behind the faces. I closed each meeting with that little ritual, by asking them how they were going to leave their mark while they worked in this building.

After the Camino, I look for inspiration from the past in my new career as a writer. One of my hobbies is researching the history of my ancestors in my family tree. From that research, I found that my Prince family line goes back all the way to medieval Germany. My ancestor Johan immigrated to America in the 1750s with his family. Being in my forties myself, I am inspired by the guts he had to take such a bold move at age forty-one. I learned that one of my ancestors, Alexander, was a scholar and published a book in the late 1500s. I arranged a side trip to the university town that had a copy of his papers in the library. When I arrived, I was pleasantly surprised that they had the book and all the papers out for me to inspect in the reading room. Touching the same pages my direct ancestor had, five hundred years before, gave me chills. I worried about a bead of sweat from my forehead dropping on one of those pages. That feeling inspired me as I wrote my first book. Book writing is not just a new career for me, I hope it becomes a way for me to leave a legacy. I thanked my far-distant grandfather Alexander for that inspiration by including his name in the acknowledgments of my first book.

CAMINO LEADERSHIP LESSON—
GET INSPIRATION FROM YOUR PREDECESSORS.

▶ *Gather Stories from the Past*—As you transition to a new role, ask the veterans on the team about the past stories of the team. What were the big successes? What were the big failures? What lessons can you learn from both? Getting this information will provide tactical benefits to help you identify what you should and shouldn't do in the future. These stories will also give you examples of what success looks like that you can use to motivate yourself and your team.

▶ *Create Team Pride*—Stories of past challenges and successes can provide inspiration to your team. Just like with countries, history can be a force to tie people together around common interests. If you can make people feel proud to be part of your team because of an illustrious history, they may feel happier about their work.

CHAPTER 8

Appreciate Those Who Walk with You Today

Pilgrims on the Camino.

MANY PILGRIMS SAY THE CAMINO TEACHES THEM TO APPRECIATE people around them in a new way. Leah, a pilgrim from the USA, said "the Camino made me more present in my interactions with people. I listen better. I can empathize more. I can see things in others' viewpoints more clearly." Jackie from the USA "imagined all the people who have come to walk and the fact that they have a story, too. A life story, something in their story drew them to the Camino just like me." The Beatitudes of the Pilgrim printed on Camino passports issued by other countries echoes this value elegantly like this: "Blessed are you, pilgrim, if what concerns you most is not to arrive, as to arrive with others."[1]

Other pilgrims learn what other people appreciate about them. Rose, a retired teacher from South Africa, shared this story: "I became part of a 'family' walking for the two weeks, and it was such a fabulous feeling meeting up with one another at different places. We arranged that the twelve of us would try to meet up in Burgos on my last night—all twelve made it through thick and thin, and we enjoyed a magnificent church service in the Burgos Cathedral and went out to supper together. One of the 'family' stood up and thanked me for my contribution and what I had meant to him . . . followed by the rest of the group. This left me an emotional wreck, as I hadn't realized what a difference I had made in so many little ways."

I didn't realize it, but I had already started living this "Appreciate Those Who Walk with You Today" value on my first day on the Camino. Every day, I had a moment with a woman who was walking the trail alone. She was older and slower than I was, so I passed her each day. Our daily shared moment became a ritual that I looked forward to, partly to check that she was okay and able to continue her solitary pilgrimage. Every time I passed her, I exhausted my French with a "Bon jour!" and "Ça va?" She always smiled, albeit with a more tired smile each day, and replied with different words in French, which I pretended to understand. When I reached the end of the trail in Santiago, I went to the Mass for pilgrims in the cathedral. The Mass capped off a very emotional final day for everyone, with many hugs and tears. The hug that meant the most to me was the one I got from this woman whom I had gotten to know, and care about, in dozens of one-minute interactions.

Don't Judge People

Pilgrims learn to avoid judging each other on the Camino. Pilgrims come from many different backgrounds and do the Camino for many different reasons. It is difficult to make accurate assumptions about other pilgrims, so pilgrims learn to avoid them. Karen, an engineer from the USA, shared this story: "Anytime I 'judged' someone, I learned something. A fellow pilgrim, Juan, had his backpack sent ahead because he'd had a back operation and couldn't carry it. Before I learned that, I'd just thought he was perhaps lazy. Two overweight women took a bus through difficult mountainous areas so they wouldn't be hurt or pass out somewhere. That was the best they could do, and their desire was to be there, just like I was there. The irritating cyclists in one *albergue* were actually the Dutch Olympic skating team on a different sort of training regime. Every time I judged, I was put back into my place."

Every pilgrim has a most difficult day on the Camino that she learns to work through—to not count herself out. Pilgrims also learn not to count each other out. Allan, a coal miner from Australia, shared this experience: "On our first day walking up the steep rise to Orisson, we passed two people, one 'overweight' lady and a man with a very prominent limp. I remarked to my wife, 'They will never make it' . . . the two people were struggling big-time, huffing and puffing. We didn't see them again after the first day. We arrived in Santiago thirty-four days later, all pleased with ourselves. We high-fived every person we had met on the way. The very next day, yes, in walked the two people I had written off, the man with the limp and the lady who had been carrying a bit of extra weight. My wife and I cried; how wrong I had been. We hugged the two people, they didn't know why, but it certainly taught me a valuable lesson in life."

Some pilgrims take this new acceptance of others to the workplace. Jonathan, a pilgrim from Ireland, learned to "understand that everyone has a different pace of walking, which can also translate into a different pace of learning or working at our daily job."

On my first morning on the Camino, I noticed a couple ahead of me who had shopping bags in their hands, along with big packs on their backs. I took a picture to post on Facebook with a snarky comment about how they were not going to make it far like that. I had done a lot of research on what to pack and how to pack. I took a lot of pride in squeezing everything I needed for a month into a backpack. I realized that this picture gave me an excuse to brag about my packing prowess to my Facebook friends.

Several hours later, I was sitting at the top of a hill with my backpack off, taking a too-long rest. The climb was steeper than I'd expected, and I had tweaked my ankle by stepping on a loose stone. I was less than halfway done for the day and was much more tired than I had expected to be. I was questioning whether I had bitten off more than I could chew with this trip. I finally got my courage up and started packing. Just as I had packed my water and snack back into my pack, the couple with the shopping bags appeared. They, too, were exhausted. We greeted each other with "Buen Camino!" I lingered to watch, curious to see if they were going to ditch the bags. The man pulled a camera from one of his bags and walked up to me. Even though I couldn't understand the language he was speaking, his gestures were clearly asking me to take a picture for them. I took several pictures and returned the camera. He was grateful and then made a motion to see if I wanted him to take a picture of me. He also took several. Then, seeing that I didn't have any water or snacks out, he offered me one of his snacks. I politely declined and waved good-bye, and we all said "Buen Camino."

I felt horrible for the snarky picture I had taken of them that morning. I was ashamed that I'd felt the need to cut someone else down to make me feel bigger. Why would I ever root against someone else who had not done anything against me? I still feel ashamed of my Facebook post about the couple earlier that day. At least it became a powerful teaching moment for me.

CAMINO LEADERSHIP LESSON—
DON'T JUDGE PEOPLE.

▸ *Recognize It*—If you hear yourself saying something critical about someone, ask yourself if you are being judgmental. Just because a person is doing it differently doesn't mean he is doing it incorrectly.

▸ *Think of What You Don't See*—If you find yourself judging someone, stop. Instead of thinking about what you do notice about a person, think about the things you don't know about him. What struggles and disadvantages might he have that you do not?

▶ *Address What's Behind Your Need to Judge*—If you are judging a person, you might be exposing an insecurity of your own. Do you feel threatened by her in some way? Do you worry about having the same struggle yourself?

Choose Who You Walk With

Walking the Camino is like rafting down a river of people. If a pilgrim goes at the same speed as pilgrims around her, she stays in the same crowd. If she changes her pace, she ends up with a new crowd. Since the Camino is a one-way walk, she may never again see passing pilgrims. If she wants to be around different people, she can follow this advice from Michael, a retired military officer from Ireland: "If when walking you are not too fond of your walking companion, stop and tie your shoelace. If they do not get the hint that you want to be alone, tie the other one. But remember that it works both ways and they may do the same to you."

Pilgrims learn it's okay to move through relationships with other pilgrims. "Texas" Tim, an auto dealer from the USA, summed it up this way: "Relationships have seasons. Sometimes we walk past the season designed for moving on from a relationship. Letting go is okay, and extending can lead to toxicity. It was a great lesson." Wendy, an entrepreneur from Australia, put it this way: "I do feel that the old saying 'people come into your life for a reason, a season, or a lifetime' is very true with the Camino. *Peregrinos* come from varied walks of life, and certainly from different parts of the world. We share an important snapshot of our lives during the walk and maybe for a few weeks afterwards, and then we branch off onto our own paths. But I have been forever changed from some of the lovely conversations and experiences."

Changing your crowd in the real world is more difficult, often requiring a new job. I've received many calls from executive recruiters in my career. One time I ended up taking the job offered. I wasn't looking to move from my job at the time, but the offer was too good to be true. I started the new job and knew within the first weeks that I had made a mistake. My boss and the company were fine, the job was just entirely wrong for me. I didn't like it and didn't see myself being able to succeed. I told my boss I had made a mistake and was going to leave. I asked him how long he needed me to continue to give him time to find a replacement. He surprised me when he said he wanted me for another three months. I think he didn't believe I was going to leave. I stayed through and worked hard to get my main project to a good handoff point. We parted on good terms.

That move was painful. It took me a while to find a new job. I was too embarrassed by my mistake to go back to my old employer. I had a hard time explaining it to prospective employers. But looking back, I can see that it was the right thing to do. I had made a mistake. It was better to fix it quickly than let it fester over time and set me back even more.

Early on in my Camino, I became fast friends with a woman who had brought her little dog with her. The first day or two were great, as the dog had a blast chasing butterflies as he bounded ahead of us on a nice cool day. The next day, in the hot sun, the poor dog lagged behind us and stopped to cool off in any puddle he could find along the way. It became clear to me that the dog's life would be in danger if he continued to walk the hundreds of miles more she planned. When the woman kept avoiding my advice to change her plans, I had to make the most dramatic statement one *peregrino* can make to another: I told her I would end our friendship and not walk with her anymore if she didn't take care of the dog. She wouldn't, so I did, and a couple of days later I heard from other pilgrims that she had taken the dog back home.

Later on my Camino, an older professor who was walking alone asked if he could join me. I agreed. We small-talked our way until the trail came to a small village with a large church. When we walked in, the beauty of the church interior stunned me—much more opulent and beautiful than I'd expected for a small village. Ever since I read Ken Follett's *Pillars of the Earth*, I see grand old buildings as monuments to the working people who built them more than the rich people who commissioned them. I shared that thought with my walking partner. He replied by telling me that these buildings represented exploitation, not exaltation, and lectured me on all the evils of organized religions. I sensed that this was a lecture that had been seeking an audience. I decided not to engage him in debate. His Camino was to be a different Camino than mine. At our lunch break, I took just enough extra rest and Wi-Fi time to make him decide to go on his way without me. Instead of continuing with him and wishing I were somewhere else, I just went somewhere else. That decision saved me angst. It also gave him the opportunity to keep looking for someone who was interested in hearing his point of view.

CAMINO LEADERSHIP LESSON—
CHOOSE WHO YOU WALK WITH.

▸ *Be Wary of Negative Ned*—In some workplaces, there is a difficult team member—"Negative Ned"—just waiting to latch on to newcomers joining the team. Ned has an attitude that has prevented him from forming friendships with other members of his team. He sees newcomers as opportunities. Ned wants to get a newcomer in his orbit long enough to make it uncomfortable for the newcomer to leave. Be wary of people who seek to monopolize your time in the first days at a new job.

▸ *Do "Meet & Greets"*—When you start on a new team, schedule "meet & greet" meetings with everyone else on your team and other stakeholders. The agenda should just be to get to know each other. You have a window of opportunity as the new person to schedule a meeting like that. Take advantage of it to widen your social circle early in your new job.   The easiest, least painful way to break with someone negative is to build relationships with others.

Nurture Acquaintances into Relationships

One of the best parts of the Camino experience is meeting many new people, from many different places and backgrounds, in a short time. The Camino can be an unparalleled networking opportunity if you take advantage of it. Karen from the USA "learned that if I felt something, wanted to tell someone something, I'd better do it now; I might not see that person again. I wanted to bring this to my 'real life'." Oihana, a special needs assistant in Ireland who has done three different Camino routes, learned how to keep in touch with pilgrims she met. "I bring a notebook and a pen to record the important moments, emails, phones, or addresses of people I meet on the route, and send them photos after. Some of them replied and continue with the contact, others no. It's normal in life, but I try to be very good at keeping up with relationships." Arminelle, a storyteller from Australia, learned to see new relationships in a new way: "While walking, I had days where I walked with someone for only one day but we had such interesting conversations on that one day that they have stayed with me forever. Now I can better enjoy people for the time we spend together rather than judging a relationship based on the length of time spent together."

In my life off the Camino, I've had about a dozen different jobs since college. Switching jobs this many times has its pluses and minuses. One of the biggest benefits is meeting new people. Every new job made me part of a new network. When I look at my networks on my social media profiles, I am amazed at how many different networks and cities into which I have connections.

Social networks like LinkedIn are great for keeping updated contact information on all the people you meet in your career. They are much better than the manual address books of old. More importantly, however, they are also great ways to maintain relationships with old colleagues. At a minimum, I take the time to reach out to people whenever I get a notice about their birthday or professional event like a job change.

My Camino experience taught me how my efforts to nurture relationships with old colleagues could pay off in a big way. I was in the middle of my Camino along the long desolate *meseta* when I stopped at a café for lunch one day. I took out my iPhone and tested for a Wi-Fi signal. They had one and I checked my messages. One of them was quite unexpected: it was from a training manager in the USA who needed my help.

Before I left for the Camino, I had laid some groundwork for my next job in the "real world" when I got back. I was going to start a training business I had long wanted to do. To get a head start, I launched a starter version of my website before I left for the Camino. I planned to start promoting my website when I got back, but did nothing before that. The website was just parked out there waiting for me to get back.

I read the email from the training manager. She had put together a training program for dozens of people in her company. It was part of an academy that they were launching for high-potential staff. One of the trainers she had booked had backed out at the last moment. She found my website and wanted to see if I could fill in. She was in quite a bind, as the training was a specialty not many people do. The good news was I was experienced in training that niche skill—the problem-solving and communication methodology that the top strategy consultants use. The bad news was that she needed the trainer to be in Hawaii in one week to teach the class. She asked if I was available and if I could get her a proposal right away.

As I sat looking at my backpack and dusty boots, several emotions went through my head. I was excited to get an unexpected good start to my business. I was distraught that I didn't have the bandwidth, literally and figuratively, to respond to her appropriately. Even though I had never met this woman, her email made me want to help her. I was about to email her back with an "I am so sorry, but I am on the Camino and can't help you" when I remembered an old colleague named Mike Figliuolo. Mike and I had worked at the same bank for a while years ago. As former strategy consultants, we were two of the handful of people who taught a class like this for the bank. We'd never worked together or even met, but we knew each other by reputation. We had both left the bank years before, but I'd made a point to keep in touch with him about once a year. Mike had launched his own training business, *thought*LEADERS LLC, and I knew he taught the classes the woman needed. I forwarded the email to him and asked him if he could help.

When I got to my *albergue* at the end of the day, I checked my email again. Not only had Mike responded that he could help the woman out, he'd put together a proposal to send her. He didn't have the days open to do the training himself, but he found one of his other qualified trainers who could do it on the short notice. I connected Mike and the training manager via email, and they ended up making the training work. It went so well that they wanted a second session of the training a couple of months later. That time, I was able to go out to Hawaii and deliver it myself.

The story didn't end there. Mike and I enjoyed working with each other so much that we decided to continue the partnership. A week or two later, I was still on the Camino walking through a particularly beautiful mountain stretch near O Cebreiro, when another request came into my website for a training session. This time it wasn't short notice, but it was from even farther away—from the Middle East. I forwarded that request to Mike, and he was able to turn the request into a contract and training dates that I delivered several months later.

So looking back, the small investment of time and effort I had made to keep in touch with Mike over the years was one of the best investments I've ever made.

CAMINO LESSON—
NURTURE ACQUAINTANCES INTO RELATIONSHIPS.

▸ *Connect on Social Networks*—When you meet a new person at work, ask him if he's on LinkedIn and would mind if you sent him a connection request. Send the request promptly. Don't follow up with him, however, if he doesn't respond. If he wants to connect, he has your connection at hand. If he doesn't respond, it may simply be that he doesn't log on often or isn't comfortable connecting.

▸ *Join or Create Alumni Groups*—If you are connected with several former colleagues from the same job, see if there is a private group for alumni of that organization on Facebook and LinkedIn. If there isn't such a group, consider launching one. Use the group to share articles and news that people in the group might find uniquely interesting.

▶ *Find Excuses to Reach Out*—Once you are connected, find meaningful ways to reach out to your connection to let him know you are thinking about him from time to time. At the minimum, when you see him start a new job, congratulate him. When he posts something you find useful, take the one second it requires to hit the "like" button or the few seconds it takes to make a comment. (They will notice.) If you see an article or post you think he would find useful, forward it to him. Don't overdo it, but you should try to reconnect in some small way with everyone in your network at least once a year.

▶ *Find Opportunities to Meet*—If you are traveling on business to another city, search your network to see who in your network lives there. Arrange a meeting if possible.

▶ *Identify Ways to Help Them*—When you hear of a job or business opportunity that is not right for you to pursue, search your network for others who might be interested. Forwarding a potential job or sale opportunity is a great way to reconnect. Your contacts will appreciate the help and be more open to future messages you send.

CHAPTER 9

Imagine Those Who Will Follow You

A section of the Camino through the meseta.

PILGRIMS WHO WALK THE CAMINO FEEL AN INHERENT DUTY TO HELP others do it, too. That has been true for pilgrims for centuries. For example, Domenico Laffi, the Italian pilgrim who walked the Camino in the 1600s and wrote a journal, described his efforts to help pilgrims following him: "From here onwards it is very easy to lose one's way because one sees nothing but empty, sandy plain. So for the benefit of poor pilgrims, I shall give directions to keep them on the right road so they do not get lost. On first arriving in this sandy waste—or any others of the same kind—when you come to two or three roads and want to know which is the right one, you will find pilgrims have made two or three heaps of stones by the side of whichever road is the right one. Likewise, on reaching a wood where there may also be two or three ways, to know which is the right one you will see that pilgrims strip the bark from two or three trees with the tip of their stave to show that this is the way to follow."[1]

When I read this value, it hit home immediately. The weight of all the pilgrims before me made me feel an enormous responsibility. The Camino felt like a thousand-year-old museum where I was allowed to touch the exhibits. There were no velvet ropes or guards separating me from the history. That made me feel personally responsible to protect this living museum. I wanted future pilgrims to experience it as I did. I also wanted to tell others about the experience so they might be inspired to follow.

Don't Ruin It for Others

I sat with thousands of people on a football field in a goofy costume on a dangerously hot May day in Philadelphia in 1996. Many of my fellow MBA students skipped the university-wide commencement ceremony because we had our own separate ceremony later that day, but I had to go to this one, too, because I was on the commencement speaker selection committee. Our commencement speaker was a celebrity, but he wasn't our dream first choice. We had our hopes set on Nelson Mandela. I didn't recall Tom Brokaw being mentioned in our committee meetings, so when we were informed he was it, I felt a bit surprised and disappointed. Evening news anchors were big deals back then, but they weren't Nelson Mandela.

Then I heard his speech.

The University of Pennsylvania holds its graduation and reunion weekends at the same time every May. That year, the Class of 1946 was convening for their fiftieth reunion, and Brokaw called them out specifically in the close of his speech. He talked about how many in that class were part of the generation who grew up in the Great Depression, won the Second World War, and then came home to build America into a superpower. Brokaw closed his speech by saying: "I am in awe of them. Fifty years from now, let another commencement speaker stand here and say of your generation, 'They saved their world. I am in awe of them.' This is your time. Take it on. . . . We're counting on you."[2]

That closing stuck with me right as I was preparing to start my own business career. I thought there was no way my generation could live up to what that generation had done. We would hopefully never face the same hardships they had to overcome. But it did plant a seed in my mind that I needed to think about the impact of my actions in my career on future generations.

It also stayed on Tom Brokaw's mind. Two years later, Brokaw published a book called *The Greatest Generation*. Without announcing it, he'd been giving us a sneak peek at a future best-selling book that would help give that generation a name and special recognition.

My walk one early morning on the Camino started with an interesting twist. I was walking alone in a remote stretch between two villages. A young man approached me and asked me in Spanish if I had seen any police. Even though I was taken aback by the question, I sensed he wasn't a threat. I replied back in Spanish I had not seen any police. He thanked me and then jogged to a car parked on the side of a street and drove away.

I started to piece together the experience when I saw the first piece of litter on the side of the path. The trash was a weird mix of orange rinds and wine bottles. There had obviously been a big party here the night before. The young man must have just finished sleeping off the aftereffects and was worried about getting pulled over if he drove.

As I continued walking, the amount of litter increased all the way to the next little town. When I saw the first decorations, I realized that the town had had their annual festival the night before. In Spain, towns often have patron saints, and they celebrate with a big party on the day their patron saint is remembered in the Catholic calendar. I missed quite the party. If only I had stretched my walk the day before by a few more miles, I thought, I would have had quite a fun night.

The real insight I got from that memory was the litter. It made me realize that I had not noticed much litter on the Camino. I had not seen any pilgrims doing any littering. I saw some picking up litter they found. Pilgrims generally make sure they don't ruin the Camino for future pilgrims.

Good leaders also avoid ruining things for people who follow them. They consider how their actions today shape possibilities tomorrow. When I was a senior executive, I knew I would move on someday and leave the role to a successor. I felt obligated to leave the role in at least as good a shape as I had inherited it.

I developed a mental picture to help remind me to be thoughtful of how my actions would impact the future. I pictured myself coming back to my organization in twenty years as a visitor at an anniversary party. I pictured myself sitting in the auditorium, listening to the speeches. I imagined studying the faces of the staff in the audience. Did they look inspired by their mission, or bored by their jobs? Did they represent the community they served? Did their leaders talk *at* them, or communicate *with* them? The organization I was part of had great energy, and I wanted to make sure that would still be true twenty years later. That vision of success helped keep me focused as I made decisions.

CAMINO LEADERSHIP LESSON—
DON'T RUIN IT FOR OTHERS.

▸ *Create a Vision of the Future*—Imagine your team ten or twenty years in the future. What do you hope it looks like? Does it still exist? Has it been lifted or buried by changes in technology? Is it a fun place to work? Does it have a proud history that makes it an attractive place to work? Once you have a vision for what a good future looks like, you can start assessing your actions today as contributing to or detracting from that future.

▸ *Financial Planning*—Put your team's house in financial order today so you aren't handicapping its future. Analyze and forecast your cost structure. If your costs are growing too fast, start curbing them now. Assess your infrastructure against future needs. Plan to update or replace it. You may be long gone by the time the benefits of these actions take place, but you owe it to your team to be a steward of their future.

▸ *Think About Precedents You Are Setting*—Every decision you make as a leader becomes a precedent for future decisions. It is tempting to take a shortcut or make an exception to the rules to get something done. But every time you bend the rules, you are weakening them and exposing yourself to claims of favoritism. Every time you don't take advantage of something you have a right to, you are weakening future claims. You owe it to your successors to leave them with the same authorities and options you have now.

Show the Way

Pilgrims help pilgrims coming behind them on the trail. Sandy from the USA described her own efforts to help those behind her: "I have always thought about those who will follow me, and while on the Camino I tried to observe some small way I could make the trip easier for those coming after me. I bought fly traps and put them up in a hostel near a field that was overrun with flies. I bought a surge protector for a hostel that only had one. I left a blank journal on the bed I left the first day, with a note that said 'this is for you.' I left some Compeed in a hostel for people with blisters like mine." People who live along the Camino also help maintain the trail. Pearl from New Zealand remembers, "Walking the Roman roads and ancient paths always reminded us of the significance of what we were doing. In one section, a chap personally cared for it by removing any rubbish and painting the yellow arrow markers regularly— that made us proud to walk 'his' section. Now I look around and often think of those who have forged the way and what it cost them and how hard it was so that we can appreciate it now."

On every project I worked on as a management consultant, my favorite day was the last day. Projects typically ended with a big final meeting with the senior-most executives at the client. We would present our work and recommendations via a slide presentation. If we had done our job well, we would persuade the client to accept our recommendations. After weeks or months of hard work, the final meeting gave us a sense of closure. We felt like celebrating.

On the other hand, one of my least favorite days came right after the end of a project. We had to write up a summary of the project to put in our firm's knowledge repository. These summaries formed an important part of the consulting firm's intellectual capital. Whenever I started a new project, I searched the repository for any similar projects in the past to get a head start. It was a valuable resource.

The irony was that the summary I had to write would never be of any use to me. I already knew the history with that project because I'd lived it. I viewed the summary as a hassle. Many other consultants must have as well, because managers had to frequently nag people to complete those write-ups. Partners were measured on the completion rate of summaries for all the projects they were responsible for. The firm would also withhold any funds for any end-of-the-project celebration until the summary was done. The summaries always got completed, but it often took a lot of nagging.

After I got back from my Camino, I found many websites and groups on Facebook about the Camino. I was impressed with how active and helpful people who had already done the Camino were on those sites. It seemed like every message from a prospective *peregrino* generated a lot of helpful advice and encouragement from people around the world. I'd researched many trails using the internet over the years, but nothing compared to the sense of community around the Camino. The former pilgrims were not there to gloat about how they had done a challenge relatively few others have done. They were there to cheer on newcomers.

When I was walking the Camino, the biggest boost I got from pilgrims ahead of me came in the form of graffiti along the way with messages to encourage pilgrims. I am not a fan of graffiti, but it was different on the Camino. It wasn't the typical "tagging" or common vandalism like you see in many modern cities. This graffiti was more like poetry. I remember seeing the simple phrase "Super Victor" with a simple "go" or an arrow scratched in signs along the way. While I realized they were probably written by or for another person named Victor, they did make me smile and realize how far I had come. Many other graffiti tags were left as encouragement for other pilgrims to continue on through the pain that piles on pilgrims after weeks of fifteen-mile days. They seem to be strategically placed just before a long upward climb or after a long stretch between villages.

When I got back from the Camino, I decided to encourage others to do it. I wrote blogs about the lessons I'd learned on my Camino that would help me in my work life. I was surprised when my first Camino blog got selected by LinkedIn's editors to be promoted to their larger network. Within a day, it was one of the top three articles on LinkedIn's blogging platform, right between Sir Richard Branson and Arianna Huffington's latest posts. It got thousands of reads and hundreds of likes. I followed up with two more blogs that had an equal impact.

The feedback I got made me realize that I could help people discover the Camino through my writing. It encouraged me to start shopping my lessons from the Camino as a book idea.

After many months of selling the book proposal and writing the manuscript, you are reading the results.

CAMINO LEADERSHIP LESSON—
SHOW THE WAY.

▸ *Record Your Lessons Learned*—Future generations can only learn the lessons of past generations if those lessons are recorded. You should help your successors by recording your lessons. Such records can go by many different names, ranging from the benign "after-action report" to the dark "post-mortem." Whatever you call them, ensure your team is doing them.

▸ *Market Your Lessons*—Having a record of your experience is only useful if people know it is available. Publish your lessons so anyone who might benefit can see them. Advertise your lessons.

▸ *Be a Mentor*—Offer your time to people who are years behind you on a career. Structure your mentorship to make it productive. If someone wants you to mentor them, put the onus on her to make it a productive relationship. Have her organize meetings with you. Give her homework. Mentoring can be a great way to help people, but only if both parties invest the time and effort to treat it seriously.

Don't Compete with Successors

Pilgrims learn to resist the temptation to compare Camino experiences with others who follow. Arminelle, a storyteller from Australia, described it this way: "Something that I heard time and time again on the Camino was, 'It's your Camino'—

meaning you can do it however you want. I think about this often. Every person has their own path, their own way through life; and if we respect that, we will all get on so much better." Pam from the USA described it this way: "What the Camino helped me to recognize is that we are all walking this journey called life. We are heading in the same direction toward the same destination but doing it a little differently. There is no right or wrong way to walk this journey, but there will be lessons and blessings along the way, depending on our path." Rosie from Australia summed it up this way: "We thought about those who had been before us and all those who would come after us, all on the same journey, but it would affect every one of us differently."

My job working for the mayor ended when he lost his reelection bid. We had a long transition period before the new mayor would start. While the campaign had been bitter, we wanted to make sure the transition was successful. The services local governments provide, such as police, fire, and child protection services, are too important to fumble during a transition. I was tasked to lead the effort to get every city agency to prepare a briefing book that would help the mayor-elect and his team hit the ground running. Despite being on my way out of the job, I treated the task with the same rigor I treated everything else in the job. We prepared an outline of all the information we would give on each agency. With dozens of agencies accounting for almost $10 billion in spending, the amount of data was huge. When printed out, it filled several binders and boxes. Instead of just doing a "data dump," we invested time to put the data into charts that best conveyed the underlying picture. We also asked the agencies to be frank about identifying the problems they were facing. After an enormous amount of work, we delivered the transition briefing books to the new mayor's team far ahead of their inauguration date. It was so big, we needed a dolly to carry all the boxes into their office. I imagined getting many questions and meeting requests to help digest it.

I don't think any of it was ever used. I was frustrated, but I later understood. The new mayor and team wanted a fresh start. That is the whole reason they ran to unseat the mayor. They had a mandate from the voters to lead their own way.

Pilgrims do the Camino in their own way and for their own reasons. I learned this while I walked with others. Even though I am competitive by nature, I learned to avoid comparing others' Camino experience to mine, as in being better or worse.

After I completed my Camino and returned home, many people reached out to ask for advice about doing it. I enjoyed giving advice but was careful not to be too prescriptive or descriptive. I didn't want to play the spoiler about the surprising experiences. I also didn't want to be the domineering person who pushed them to replicate my Camino. I decided I would provide as much help as I could to inspire a trip and to prepare for it, but would stop there. Once a friend started a Camino, I wanted her to experience it without any interference from me.

That same lesson is valuable for leaders as well. At some point, all leaders turn over the reins to another leader—either voluntarily or involuntarily. You should treat transitions out of a role as thoughtfully as you treat transitions into a role. *Be helpful and available to your successor, but don't get in their way.*

CAMINO LEADERSHIP LESSON—
DON'T COMPETE WITH SUCCESSORS.

▸ *Transition Out Like You Were Transitioning In*—If you know your successor, ask her what she wants. If you don't know your successor, prepare a briefing you can leave that focuses on what you think she needs to hear, not what you want to tell her. Think back to your own experience when you started in that role. What did you wish your predecessor had prepared you for? What were you not interested in hearing from her?

▶ *Make Your Closing Case*—Use your farewell message to summarize the team's achievement during your leadership and the condition in which you are leaving things. It will help you define your legacy. It will also ensure that you are not blamed unjustly for poor performance in the future.

▶ *Stay Silent*—It is natural to want to maintain relationships with your old team members. Avoid the temptation, however, to become a lightning rod that encourages them to complain about their new boss. It is nice to hear that you are missed, but shut down any comparisons between your leadership and the new boss. Think about how you would want the predecessor in your current role to interact with your new team. Less is probably more.

PART III

APPLYING LESSONS
FROM THE CAMINO

The author on the Camino near the Cruz de Ferro.

CHAPTER 10

The Post-Camino
Impact

WALKING THE CAMINO IS AN INTENSE EXPERIENCE THAT HELPS PIL-grims reflect on life. Hans from Belgium captured it this way: "The Camino is so simple, but in essence it is life in general. So much happens in a single day. Multiply this by about thirty-five days, and it felt like a small life in this larger one." Karen from the USA said, "The Camino felt like my life crammed into a very short period of time. Decisions that I made changed what would happen next, who I would meet, where I would stay."

The Camino changes many pilgrims long after the walk has ended. Valerie from Canada has been "reminded daily that the Camino 'begins at its end.' The Camino experience is something that can resonate with many aspects of one's life and has many things to teach and messages to share if you're open and still enough to hear and see them!!" Sandy from the USA calls her Camino "one of the hardest things I have ever done in my life, but it has also been the most rewarding in terms of personal growth. The person I was at the beginning of the Camino is gone, and in her place is a much brighter, loving, generous, giving woman!" Christopher, a mortgage processor from the USA, says his Camino "gave me tolerance. And in that, I returned a peaceful man."

The Camino also makes pilgrims hungry for further adventures. Donal, a pilgrim from Ireland, says his Camino "opened up a complete new life for me. I am constantly looking for new challenges." Hans from Belgium says "the Camino also made me restless. I feel there is more in this life to live up to. Now I find myself searching for more meaning and thinking about how to realize this."

I walked the Camino to take a break in my career. It turned out that my Camino was much more than a break from work; it was a career game changer for me.

The values I learned on the Camino reshaped me. I am a different person, both personally and professionally, than I was before my Camino. I find myself wishing I had learned the lessons of the Camino years before so I could have applied them in my previous leadership roles. I think I would have been a much better leader.

I can't change the past, but I have been able to change my present using the lessons I learned on the Camino. Unlike the Camino values that were given to me on my pilgrim passport, these lessons are my own, from my Camino experience. They are the result of reflections about how my life and career have changed since the Camino and how the Camino brought those changes about.

While the Camino was the way I applied these lessons, they can be applied without taking a month off, flying across an ocean, and walking across Spain. You can do these things in your own way without taking on an adventure like the Camino. The next chapters describe these lessons and then give tips on how you can get these in your own situation.

CHAPTER 11

Think About Yourself
Differently

THE COMBINATION OF PHYSICAL CHALLENGE, ALONE TIME, AND MEETING many new people makes the Camino a unique opportunity for self-examination. "Texas" Tim, a car dealer from the USA, described the introspective nature of his Camino this way: "This Camino mirrors my life. The first portion was a race. The middle froze me. The last showed me who I am, or who I am becoming. I have spent forty-five years getting here. I worked, pushed, and plowed forward. I gave time to my kids on my terms. I languished for approval from people. I bought in and woke up one morning a forty-four-year-old miserable fat man. The Camino served as a reflecting pool for me."

Find Strangers to Find Yourself

We tend to work with people like ourselves. Within an organization, we share a mission and a culture. We choose our employers, and our employers choose us, in part because we have things in common. Within a profession, we share interests, skills, and experiences with others in our field.

When you get on the Camino, the only thing you share with the other people is that you somehow are willing, able, and crazy enough to do the Camino. The Camino is like the United Nations in hiking boots, representing many countries, careers, ages, and other demographics. Because of that diversity, when someone asks you what you do for work, you may have to explain from scratch. Things like job titles, industries, and company names do not automatically convey a background as they do at home. You may also end up describing how you got into the field you are in. These discussions can provide clarifying, retrospective moments you may not previously have had. Hans from Belgium summed it up this way: "I started walking the Camino with the mind-set of figuring myself out and what I want from life (mainly work), but found myself over time thinking about the people around me, and learning about myself from who they were."

As I described my career to strangers on the Camino, I heard myself telling a story I had been living but not seeing. I had moved between six careers over the twenty-odd years since college. I had jumped from one new field that excited me to another, staying just long enough in each until the excitement wore off. Each jump made sense, but when I explained them, they didn't seem connected to a long-term career strategy. It was only on the Camino that I found the common link.

That clarifying moment came when I walked on the Camino with a Californian named Tony who described his decision to leave a career in advertising to find happiness as a high school English teacher. His story stuck with me because internet advertising had been one of the several careers I'd had in my life. I never saw myself becoming a high school teacher, but his description of the rewards of teaching connected with me. It made me want to be a teacher in some way.

Then a realization dawned on me—I had been teaching throughout my career. In fact, it was the thing I enjoyed the most in past jobs. I learned advanced analysis and communication skills early in my career. Those skills became my core strength at work. As a manager, I'd been informally teaching my team members these skills in every interaction. I'd also been a part-time trainer in these skills in my consulting and banking jobs. When I became a COO, I even launched a training program in these skills for the entire organization.

The Camino gave me an epiphany—the training business I was starting was my calling, not just my next move. And to make sure I got the message, the Camino even delivered two clients to launch the business while I was walking the path.

When I got home, I finished launching my training business, DiscoveredLOGIC.com, and I haven't looked back. I've trained organizations across thirteen time zones over the last three years and have enjoyed every second of it.

HOW TO DO THIS AT WORK:

▶ *Inventory Your Jobs*—Identify the few things in your current job you most enjoy. See which of those you also did in your previous jobs to find common threads of what most inspires you at work.

▶ *Define the Ideal Job*—Identify what a job would look like that centered on the favorite things you do. If such a job exists, research what it looks like in terms of lifestyle and compensation. Consider if you could make that work.

▶ *Join New Networks*—Meeting people who have different backgrounds and interests than yours will force you to introduce yourself in new ways. These new acquaintances will ask you questions that people in your existing networks won't ask. Target networks around hobbies, faith, sports, or other pastimes—anything other than your current job.

▶ *Connect with People in Your Target Field*—If you identify a new interest to target, connect with people in that area. For example, I often get approached by former colleagues seeking advice on how to write their first book. I did the same, so I am happy to "pay it forward" to friends who aspire to write a book. I think many authors share that feeling.

I Walked Across Spain, I Can do *That*

Most people would say walking across a country the size of Spain is crazy. It's not *technically* crazy, because thousands of people do it every year. But it is crazy in a different way, because billions of people never even consider doing it.

Doing a crazy adventure like the Camino stretches what a pilgrim thinks she can do. Joann, a cable assembly operator from the USA, said, "The Camino taught me that I have more strength in me than I would have imagined. Every day, I woke up ready to walk and by the end of the day I didn't think I would ever walk again. But walk I did . . . and prayed and cried." Donal from Ireland said, "I walked my first Camino in 2010 at the age of seventy...Walking long distances gave me a lot of confidence. I also found that I was inspirational to other people in that they learned that anything is possible if you put your mind to it. More than one person told me that I was an inspiration to them and that they wanted to be like me when they were my age."

The Camino stretched what I thought I was able to do. Part of the reason I did the Camino was because it sounded like such an achievement. I loved the idea of being able to say, "Well, there was that time I walked across Spain," in conversations for the rest of my life.

Once I finished, I found that completing the Camino gave me more than just something to boast about; it changed me in a deeper way. When I see a challenge now, I put it in perspective: "If I was able to walk across Spain, I can surely do that."

It also gives me a bigger appetite to take on new challenges. One of the things on my "bucket list" had been to write a book, but I had been too intimidated to even start. After I got back from the Camino, though, I decided to try. I had a leadership concept I had been forming over my years of leading teams. In all the alone time walking the Camino, I was able to think deeply about it and sharpen it. When I got home, I started to put the concept down on paper. The paper turned into a detailed outline of a dozen pages or so. I didn't know what it took to write a book, but I knew someone who did. I called Mike Figliuolo, the same guy who helped me serve the clients who came to me while I was on the Camino. He'd published a successful book, so I asked him if my outline had book potential. He said it did and offered to coauthor it with me. Eighteen months later, our book, *Lead Inside the Box: How Smart Leaders Guide Their Teams to Exceptional Results,* was published. It got nice reviews from several big-name publications. It was named a Top 20 Leadership Book of 2016 by *Leadership and Management Book Review.* It got picked up by selective retail outlets like Hudson Booksellers and FedEx Office. What had seemed like an impossibility before the Camino had come true.

That first book would never have happened if I had not gotten the burst of confidence I got by completing the Camino. The Camino provides long after you finish, if you let it.

HOW TO DO THIS AT WORK:

▶ *Inventory Past Accomplishments*—What "impossible" challenges have you overcome in the past from which you can draw confidence? These challenges can come from your personal or professional life, and from all ages. For example, I still draw strength dealing with difficult people today by remembering when I successfully stood up to bullies as a kid.

▸ *Get Inspired by Peers' Accomplishments*—Some people see school reunions as a chance to compare resumes. I see them as a chance to find inspiration from past peers. The most inspiring are the ones who found a passion later in life and successfully pursued it. If one of my high school classmates can make it as a director in Hollywood, maybe I'm not as crazy as I thought to want to write books.

▸ *Vacation with Purpose*—Your vacations can be more than just time off; they can be great personal-development opportunities to prove you can do things you didn't think you could. If you use your off time to conquer a challenge, you will find yourself stronger for it, not just personally but also professionally. If you need extra vacation flexibility from your employer, make the case that you will be getting professional development from your request.

▸ *Bring Outside Experiences in to Work*—Think about the challenges you have overcome in areas outside of work. Use those to put the challenges you face at work into perspective. "If I can [insert challenge overcome,] I can do this!"

Be More Than Your Job

Whatever a pilgrim does in life outside the Camino matters little on the Camino. "Pilgrim" is the only vocation that matters for people walking the Camino. Arminelle from Australia put it this way: "I also found it fascinating how unimportant your professional life is on the Camino. Most of the people I met made a point of not asking and not telling what they did for a living, and this was empowering. We could no longer hide or be judged on our profession, but rather on who we were as people. For some people, this seemed to be a major hindrance—they

THE CAMINO WAY   133

needed everyone to know that they were a hotshot lawyer—and all I could think was how sad that people can only define themselves by what they do."

I lived in San Diego, California for a couple of years while I was in my midthirties. I was transferred out there by my employer, a large bank on the East Coast. The bank had purchased a dot-com company in San Diego and wanted to bring in some management from the new parent company. I felt like I had won the lottery when I got the call about the move. It was a great role, with a nice relocation package and more money. Most importantly, it was in San Diego, home of perfect weather and beautiful beaches.

Two short years later, I was back on the East Coast, working in Washington, DC. The bank had decided to move the operation from San Diego to Texas, at which point I chose to transfer to a different job with the same company in the Washington, DC, headquarters.

I had lived in DC before and loved it, but moving back was a shock. I missed the San Diego weather and beaches. I also missed San Diego's laid-back culture about work. In San Diego, people often wore shorts and flip-flops to work and generally didn't work late hours either. There's too much life to live outside of work when you live in a paradise like San Diego.

When I got back to Washington, DC, it seemed like everyone asked me where I worked within seconds of meeting me. Only then did I realize many of my friends in San Diego had *never* asked me what I did for work. They only cared if I *was* good company, not if I *worked for* one. That difference drove home to me how the two cultures were different. In San Diego, work is something a person does. In Washington, work is who a person *is*.

I soon got caught up in that Washington mind-set. I became focused on where my employer and job title placed me in the

DC social hierarchy. While feigning modesty, I loved telling people about my job, particularly as my job titles sounded more impressive, at least to me.

The Camino helped me realize that I had to be more than my job title to be good company. People didn't care about what I had done off the Camino. They just cared if I brought them good energy on the Camino. I took that to heart when I got back home. Work became just one part of me again. I wanted to be better at my other roles in life, as a family member, friend, and partner.

HOW TO DO THIS AT WORK:

▸ *Don't Immediately Ask About Work*—Make a mental note on how you do introductions with new people. Do you quickly ask newcomers about their jobs, no matter what the setting? Ask your spouse or friend if you do.

▸ *Assess Your Behavior*—Think of a time when you asked that question out of context. Why did you ask? Were you trying to get them to ask you the same question so you could demonstrate where you were on a social hierarchy?

▸ *Identify Yourself Differently*—When someone asks you, "What do you do," think about a better answer than just your job. "I'm a dad, husband, kids' basketball coach, and a bank executive" makes you sound more interesting and rounded than "I'm a Senior Vice President of Invoice Processing at ACME Worldwide's Widget Division." Introducing yourself in a more rounded way can be a good way to remind yourself to keep balance between your roles, too.

▸ *Build Your Own Brand*—Some people who work for well-known organizations rely on that as a personal brand. "I work for Megacorp" is an easy way to answer a question about work, but it can be a crutch. Think about what you would say if you no longer worked for your current employer. Imagine yourself as a professional consultant in your field of expertise and your employer as just one of your current clients. How would you describe yourself then?

▶ *Don't Conflate Jobs with Results*—Thomas Jefferson was the United States of America's third president, second vice president, and first Secretary of State. He was the second governor of Virginia. He is one of only three US presidents memorialized on both Mt. Rushmore and in the core of Washington, DC. Yet Jefferson specified that the epitaph on his tombstone should be only this: "Here was buried Thomas Jefferson, Author of the Declaration of American Independence, of the Statute of Virginia for religious freedom & Father of the University of Virginia." Jefferson didn't want to be remembered for any job he had, but only for the results he achieved. At just 173 characters, Jefferson squeezed his historic career into a "tweet-sized" summary of results. What would you like your "tombstone tweet" to say?

CHAPTER 12

Think About Others Differently

THE CAMINO IS AN INTENSE EXPERIENCE IN MEETING MANY NEW PEOPLE, from many different places, in a short time. Pilgrims are exposed to many different cultures and languages. For me, it rivaled the culture shock from my first weeks of college, when I was a Midwestern teenager from a suburban high school starting at a big-city East Coast university. The Camino taught me to think differently about others in three ways.

Look Past Nationalities

The Camino experience is beyond multinational—it's "anational." Nationalities don't matter much on the Camino. Everyone shares a common mission—to complete the pilgrim journey. For most, that means reaching Santiago de Compostela on foot. Everyone also shares the sense of adventure—or insanity—that embarking on such a mission requires. "Texas" Tim summed the feeling up this way: "I will miss communing with people from all over the world: sharing food, hearts, thoughts, hopes, dreams, and life stories with strangers from strange lands. Foreign, yet family. Gathering for reasons that vary, yet a common bond tying all together. The Camino. I will miss that."

Andi, a poker dealer from the USA, experienced international teamwork in a dramatic fashion on her Camino: "I arrived in Samos around noon. I ran into another Camino friend there, and we spent the afternoon together. As we were eating, we noticed

some clouds rolling in, and a few raindrops started to fall just as
we were paying the check. By the time we got back to our bunks
at the *albergue*, it was pouring rain and thundering. By the time
we put our wallets away, it was torrential, end-of-days, Noah's
ark type of raining, along with the loudest thunder-and-light-
ning show I had ever heard. So much rain fell so fast that the *albergue* started to flood. Water was pouring in through the doors,
and we scrambled to get all of our stuff up onto the bunks. By
the time the storm ended, there was probably eight inches of
water inside the *albergue*. The rest of the night was spent bailing
out the room, as there were no drains. This was an international
effort of epic proportions. Americans, Aussies, Italians, Ger-
mans, Spanish . . . it didn't matter, everyone was the same in the
bucket brigade. As they helped us bail out and clean the room,
the locals (monks and others who stopped by to help) said it was
the worst storm they had ever seen. By 10 P.M. or so, we had the
water out, the floor (sort of) mopped, and folks were ready to
sleep. It was still damp and humid in the room, but we were dry
for the most part. It's a day I'll never forget, not because of the
terrible flood, but because of the way everyone came together. It
demonstrated perfectly one of the best parts of the Camino to
me . . . there are no nations or borders on the Camino; everyone
is a pilgrim, no matter their country of origin or ethnicity. Giving people common goals can bridge differences!"

If people do get labels on the Camino, it is more for the way
they get to Santiago than where they started. The only critical
label I heard earned on the Camino was "He's the snorer." That
was about a man who kept other *peregrinos* up at nights with
his loud snoring in the shared sleeping quarters in the hostels. I
didn't know his name, nationality, or anything else about him
other than that he snored. I think my reputation on the Camino
centered on my big green hat with a funny-looking homemade
sunshade in the back. I know because I once lost the sunshade,

and three wonderful Belgian women knew exactly to whom to return it.

Since the Camino, I've learned to discount the importance of nationalities as well. In my personal life, I have found myself shuttling between the USA and Europe for the last three years to keep up a relationship with an amazing woman I met on my Camino. That experience has taught me that our cultures are much more similar than different. The differences present opportunities to learn rather than challenges.

I've learned that nationalities don't matter much in my work life as well. My training business is a niche, but it's a global niche. I get inquiries from around the world. When I work with potential clients, I focus more on their needs than their nationalities. I am amazed at how training rooms full of students feel more similar than different, even in very different cultures. I remember my students more for their energy and questions than their nationalities.

In short, the Camino taught me to look past nationalities and see people through the lens of shared interests and goals. Doing so has dramatically opened up my field to build business and friendships.

HOW TO DO THIS AT WORK:

▶ *Find Shared Goals and Values*—If you work with colleagues in other countries, cultural differences can make teamwork more difficult. To cut through that, identify the goals and values you share. While you might come from different cultures, you self-selected to work for the same organization. Identify what about your organization most appealed to you. For example, if "innovation" is a common thread, go back to it when cultural differences get in the way of teamwork.

▸ *Celebrate Differences as Team-Building*—Cultural differences can provide opportunities for team-building. Working in international teams provides rare opportunities to interact with people from other countries at more than a superficial level. "Team-building" activities can often feel artificial and forced. Teaching each other about customs, food, and other national differences can be a more natural way for team members to get to know each other.

▸ *Learn from Your Own International Roots*—Researching my family tree gave me a new appreciation for when I meet other nationalities at home. All my ancestors came to my country as immigrants. Some came as religious pilgrims from England in the 1600s, some as indentured servants from Germany in the 1700s, and some as economic immigrants from Eastern Europe in the 1900s. I respect the guts my ancestors must have had to come to—and the hard work ethic they needed to thrive in—America. I also think some kind locals must have helped my immigrant ancestors along the way. The Pennsylvania farmers to whom my German ancestors were indentured must have been kind, for example, because they were godparents to my first German ancestor to have been born in America. That kindness to newcomers is something I try to practice as well.

You Are Always on Some Team

Some pilgrims start the Camino in a group. Some start the Camino alone but join other pilgrims to form a group. These groups provide company and mutual support. Karen, from the USA, summarized her experience this way: "We worked as a team, and as individuals at the same time. We hiked together, we hiked apart, we met up again and were ecstatic to see each

THE CAMINO WAY 143

other. We never felt obligated in any way, but wanted to help each other if the need was there, and we let others be totally free in what they needed to do. Life should be like that."

Some pilgrims get support from groups they belong to off the Camino who have a presence along the Camino. For example, Lysa, the paramedic from England, describes how she got support from her professional counterparts along the Camino: "Ambulance volunteers shut up the ambulance station just so they could walk me to a cheap place to stay. I slept in ambulance stations, hospitals, convents, and strangers' homes. I was given care, food, shelter, and support out of the goodness of people's hearts."

Some pilgrims find a team to join before they even leave for the Camino. Maryanne, from the USA, shared her story: "When I decided to do it, I couldn't find a soul who wanted to do it with me, let alone anyone who had heard of it. So I went online and found a great group called Spanish Steps. What a gift to find like-minded Walking Souls!"

Writing a book is the hardest thing I've ever done. It's a long, tedious process that challenges and scares me. I had an experienced coauthor, Mike, for my first book. He taught me how to turn a book idea into a reality. I knew I would miss Mike's company on this book, but I knew I had to tell this story alone.

It turned out that I was not going to be writing this book alone, however. I wanted to include stories of other *peregrinos*, so I posted a survey on Facebook and targeted it at people interested in the Camino. The survey received over a hundred responses from former *peregrinos* around the world. I knew the stories would be a nice addition to the book. The gift I didn't expect was all the support and good energy that also came in from that survey. That support helped me tremendously. It was like having a hundred co-authors. I feel like I have made a hundred new friends around the world in the process as well.

HOW TO DO THIS AT WORK:

▸ *Identify Your Team*—Even when you are working alone, you are part of some team that can support you. It may be family or friends. It may be current or past colleagues. Or it may be others in your same profession. Figure out what community you are in and how to get connected.

▸ *Share with Your Team*—Tell your team about your goals and the reasons you are pursuing them. Share your experience. Set up ways people can follow your updates if they choose. While writing this book, for example, I built a group on Facebook about this book where hundreds of people track my progress and encourage me.

▸ *Include Your Family on Your Work Team*—Appreciate how your family makes your work possible. My brother, for example, was kind enough to take several other responsibilities off of my plate as my book deadline approached so I could maximize my time writing.

▸ *Appreciate Your Team*—Make sure your team knows that you appreciate the support. Whenever you get a chance, recognize people who helped you. Books have acknowledgment sections and awards have acceptance speeches where you can do that. Find, or create, channels like that to thank your team.

Uniforms Are Powerful

Pilgrims on the Camino are easy to identify, even when they're walking in a crowd of non-pilgrims. The backpacks, boots, and other hiking gear form today's pilgrim uniform. Function beats fashion in pilgrim gear. Brands and labels don't matter and do not serve as symbols of wealth or status. Karen from the USA put it this way: "When we were out there, everyone was truly equal. We looked pretty much the same. We were doing the same thing and we could be homeless or very wealthy and it didn't really matter, and no one could tell by looking at us. I just wish life could be like that. I've never seen true equality like that."

I've never worked in a job where I had to wear a uniform, so the Camino was my closest taste of uniform life. I loved it. Every day I wore my best clothes. What I lacked in variety, I made up for in comfort and confidence. I also loved not having to worry about changing and matching clothes. I always looked my best, even if I didn't look different.

Beyond my pilgrim uniform, I liked how everyone else's pilgrim uniform made it easy for me to interact with them. Pilgrims' uniforms don't differ much between the most expensive and fashionable and the least. Pilgrims' clothes don't give a lot of social cues about what a *peregrino's* life looks like outside the Camino. If you are going to judge a person, you have to at least talk to him first. The shared outfit also builds a sense of camaraderie among pilgrims. We could identify each other as fellow pilgrims by sight, and that made introductions much easier.

HOW TO DO THIS AT WORK:

▸ *Lead by Example*—If you are an executive and part of your organization wears uniforms, consider wearing one as well, at least at times. I have seen the power of this from a friend of mine who runs one of the largest public utilities in the USA. Unless he is on Wall Street trying to raise money for a bond, he is probably wearing the same uniform as his front-line workers.

▸ *Find Ways to Implement Uniforms*—If none of your work-force wears uniforms, find other ways to create uniforms. For example, if your sales team has company shirts to wear at trade shows, consider giving those to your other employees. You could encourage your team to all wear those at the same time, like company anniversaries or certain days of the week.

▸ *Find Substitutes for Uniforms*—If your folks don't wear a uniform, find something that does tie them together, such as an identity (ID) badge, and sport one yourself. Seeing the boss wearing the same outfit as the front-line employees can send a powerful message to the rest of the organization. It can also be a good reminder to executives about the necessity to keep the needs of the front-line employees in mind.

▸ *Celebrate Uniforms*—Display old versions of uniforms or company credentials as relics of your organization's history. If you have credentials that current top executives were issued when they first started, those could be of interest to employees.

CHAPTER 13

Act Differently

WALKING FIFTEEN MILES A DAY FOR THIRTY DAYS IN A ROW IS NOT A normal behavior. Just walking the Camino means that a pilgrim has decided to do something radically different in their life. Completing the Camino taught me to act differently in four ways.

Don't Wait for Retirement

Few of the pilgrims I met on my Camino were retired. Looking up the statistics, only 3.6 percent of the pilgrims who, like me, received a Compostela certificate in August 2013 listed their occupation as "retired."[1] While retirees are underrepresented in the summer months, they only account for about 12 percent of total Camino pilgrims receiving a Compostela in recent years.

I was impressed by all the retirees I did meet doing the Camino. They didn't strike me as being in above-average shape for their age. They had decided to do the walk when their schedules became easy in retirement, and they willed their way physically. Their bravery to try the Camino impressed me as much as the grit they displayed to keep going.

In a different way, I was even more impressed by the large majority of people who managed to do the Camino *before* their retirement schedules made it easy. Some people had jobs that gave them the ability to take a month off. I met more school-teachers than any other profession, by far, on my Camino. I met people in many other professions, too, who figured out how to do the Camino within more typical vacation schedules. Some people were doing the Camino for a week or two and planning to come back and do the rest of it in similar intervals. Others figured out a way to get a special dispensation to take a month off. Others, like me, took advantage of a transition from one job to another to sneak in an extra-long vacation.

For many people, "retirement" becomes an easy bin in which to sort all the things they also label as "bucket list." "I'll do that when I'm retired" is an easy way to postpone many things you would like to do but do not want to make the commitment to make them happen. For every one retiree on the Camino, I wonder how many retirees who wanted to do the Camino never will because they waited too long. Arminelle from Australia "met three people who were walking the Camino for people close to them who had died. They wanted to walk the Camino for them. For me, I simply appreciated that I was able to do this when so many can't." Oihana from Ireland shared her story: "I did my first Camino with a best, lifelong, friend for our thirtieth birthdays, and we promised each other to do the Portuguese coastal route from Baiona for our fortieth . . . my friend died suddenly when she was thirty-eight, but I did the Camino in her memory to celebrate our fortieth."

HOW TO DO THIS AT WORK:

▸ *Redefine Your Deadlines*—I don't like the term "bucket list" as a statement of life goals. Death is a terrible deadline. Deadlines can be powerful forcing mechanisms when they increase focus on a task when time and ability to get it done are still sufficient. That doesn't work with life goals. Our abilities tend to wane as we age. It is much better to set a "life list" of things we want to complete while we can. For goals requiring a physical element like completing the

Camino, set deadlines that are triggers alerting you when your window is closing. Instead of saying walking the Camino is on your "bucket list," say it is on your list of things to do before you can't walk a mile anymore.

▶ *Rank and Limit Your Goals*—A list of things to do in retirement can become a long, unprioritized bin of things you will never get to if you are not careful. If you do have a list, rank the items and focus on a finite number. Having a Top 5 or Top 10 list puts more focus and urgency on those goals. Setting a finite, manageable number as a cap makes it less intimidating to start taking action on the list. It also makes it easier to feel the sense of accomplishment when you check one or more items off.

▶ *Do Your List in Pieces*—If you have things you would like to do when you are retired, why not try them out in smaller pieces before you retire? If you want to do the Camino, do a week of it instead of doing one of your typical one-week vacations. Maybe you won't like it and decide to take it off your life-goals list. Or maybe you will love it and want to do even more similar adventures. If you "want to write a book" when you are retired, why not start blogging or writing short stories in your spare time while you are still working? Maybe those will turn into your book. Maybe you will find out you would rather have something else on your list.

Buy the Ticket, Then Figure Out the Rest

Planning a Camino is complex. To schedule a Camino, pilgrims have to find a sweet spot where financial and physical abilities align with an ability to take weeks off from other responsibilities. The planning can scare off potential pilgrims. Dave, an executive from the USA, shared his story about how he and his

wife decided to do the Camino: "In 2014, I thought I was successful. I had it all. I was fifty-three, had a beautiful wife, two
successful children, a nice house, and I was an executive at a
$4B firm. Then, with about one week's warning, I was let go
from my company. I had been at this firm for fourteen years,
highly stressed, worked twelve hours a day and many weekends, overweight, and traveled more than 100,000 miles a year.
I was totally unprepared for my journey. I went home to tell my
wife and to decide what to do next. I said, 'Let's make a positive
out of this; let's do a "bucket list" item now. Let's do the
Camino.' My wife looked at me as though I was crazy. 'Walk 500
miles in your shape? You don't like to walk the dog, let alone
walk 500 miles.' I said, 'Well, we have some time to plan and get
in shape. We aren't getting any younger, and if I can't make it,
we'll take the bus and have a great vacation.' The next day, we
purchased our tickets, bought good hiking shoes, and started
our journey. Two years later, in retrospect, I was lucky. This
was the best thing that could have happened to me. It was a gift
and I didn't know it."

I've done many hiking and biking vacations, and the most
stressful part has never been a physical or mental challenge on
the trail: the most stressful part of every trip is the weeks before, when I know I want to do it but can't get myself to commit to buying a ticket. I can get lost spending days searching for
the cheapest airfares and best schedules. I fear that if I pull the
trigger on one fare and schedule, a better one will show up the
next day. Inevitably, I purchase one and my stress level de-
creases enormously. Once I have the ticket, I know I am going.
I can then work through the details. Before I have the dates set,
I am working through an infinite set of possible itineraries.
Once I put stakes in the ground and set the dates, I can start
solving the details in between. And when I look back and estimate the time I spent looking for the cheapest fare versus the

money I saved, I realize I should have bought a ticket a long time before.

I've learned that my vacation starts the moment I buy the ticket. Researching options for routes and accommodations only makes sense when you have your itinerary set with a ticket. Envisioning myself on the trail each day as I plan is almost like experiencing the vacation in virtual reality before it starts. The mental vacation can start weeks before the physical one does.

HOW TO DO THIS AT WORK:

▶ *Identify Barriers*—The hardest part of any adventure like the Camino is the first step. There are countless reasons that kind of adventure is a bad idea. You can't take the time off from work or family obligations. You aren't in shape. You might not like it. You can't afford it. Once you decide you want to do something like the Camino, identify the barriers and sort them into different bins.

▶ *Create a Plan to Get Through Barriers*—The first bin is those things you can change. You can get yourself in walking shape, for example. You probably can save up cash and vacation time for the trip. Write down each barrier and identify what you need to do to get through it. Estimate the time it will take. Once you have those in writing, you have a plan and a start date.

▶ *Contingency Plan*—Then think about the things you cannot change. For example, maybe you won't like walking the Camino. Maybe you will get injured and won't be able to continue. Come up with contingency plans so you can salvage the experience.

▸ *Pull the Trigger*—Once you have a start date and contingency plans, buy the ticket. The ticket will create a black-and-white deadline to focus you to take the first step. It will also represent your commitment to do the adventure. You are no longer just talking about doing the Camino, you have a ticket to do it.

▸ *Recall Previous Leaps*—If you still don't have the confidence to pull the trigger, think back to a previous time you hesitated before a big decision. Maybe it was taking a new job. Maybe it was taking a personal relationship to the next step. Recall your mind-set at those moments to help you assess whether you are holding back for valid reasons or just nerves.

Less Is More

Pilgrims pay a lot of attention to how much their backpacks weigh because they carry them for many hours and miles every day. There is a joke that *peregrinos* know how much their underwear weighs by the end of the journey. By carrying everything I needed for a month on my back, I learned to be smart with differentiating what I needed from what I wanted. Variety in clothing colors and styles drove complexity and weight in my backpack. By the end of the first week of the trip, I found that I was using 20 percent of the clothes I'd packed 80 percent of the time, and the rest was deadweight. I ended up throwing away a lot of the "I want" clothes and just washing and wearing the "I need" clothes more.

The Camino taught something to Kailagh from New Zealand. "On day one walking over the Pyrenees, I learned a powerful lesson in materialism. We had virtually nothing in our packs anyway; but having stopped in Paris on our way, I had snuck in a few children's picture books (this is what we collected on our travels), thinking this would be no issue to carry

800 kilometers across a country! However, slogging our way over that mountain range on day one taught me that I need nothing in this life that is going to make my journey more difficult. It only made everything harder. So we left our beautiful new books in Roncesvalles and hoped some local kids might be happier because of our lightened loads. A small lesson that taught me that, really, I don't need material things to make me happy; it's just extra stuff to carry with you and only makes moving on to the next thing heavier."

Some pilgrims try to keep a minimalist approach in their life after the Camino. Karen from the USA described her Camino this way: "I had a pack, everything I could possibly need, weighed maybe fifteen pounds max, and I didn't need anything else. I tried to de-clutter when I got home, then stopped, and am now trying again to get rid of things I don't need." Pearl from New Zealand got this insight from her Camino: "Unload unnecessary baggage from your life—you can't carry it all; if it's not your responsibility, and you can't do anything about it, leave it."

I started thinking how useful a minimalist mentality could be in scoping projects in the workplace. I remembered how many new technology projects I saw got bloated by extra "nice-to-have" features. I was as guilty as anyone about adding new demands on projects. I wondered how eager I would have been to add on those new demands if I'd been the one carrying the load.

HOW TO DO THIS AT WORK:

▸ *Be Ruthless in Scoping*—As I scope future projects at work, I will ruthlessly force myself to determine what is essential to deliver well, and strip out all the "nice-to-have" parts of the project that aren't absolutely required. If I want to add something new to an established scope, I will identify something of the same size that can be removed to make room.

▸ *Choose Speed over Mass*—There is usually a trade-off between the scope of a project and the time required to complete it. There are many benefits of choosing to get a smaller scope delivered faster. You could beat a competitor to the market. It could cost less. You could quickly gain real-world experience to better define the next iteration of the project.

▸ *Live Off the Land*—It is tempting to scope projects to include every needed ingredient. That desire for complete independence from the outside world can bloat a project. One thing I liked about the Camino was the fact that I did not need to carry a tent, food, and water; I could rely on finding those needs along the way.

▸ *Pack Seeds, Not Crops*—You can apply this "less is more" approach from backpacking to communicating. Set the maximum number of pages or words your emails, blogs, or presentations should be. Pack the maximum value into that "word budget" by writing to convey ideas, not just to describe things. Write just enough about an idea for your reader to fill in the rest. Then use your remaining words to paint more mental pictures. If each picture is worth a thousand words, your words will blossom like seeds in a field.

Drop the Stone You Are Carrying

The Cruz de Ferro marks a centerpiece of the Camino for many pilgrims. It is a cross on top of the highest point on the Camino, about two weeks short of Santiago de Compostela. The cross sits atop a pile of stones that gets bigger every day. By tradition, *peregrinos* start the Camino with a stone they drop off when they get to the Cruz de Ferro. Each *peregrino* makes a ceremony of adding their stone to the pile. Many say a prayer.

Many pilgrims do the Camino to help get over some trouble that has weighed them down. For some, it is dealing with loss. For others, it is about losing unwanted baggage they have been carrying. Some pilgrims share their goal with other pilgrims to get support. Others keep it a secret. Pilgrims learn not to ask.

Several pilgrims shared their experience at the Cruz de Ferro with me. Jonathan from Ireland said, "Leaving a stone behind at some point during the walk was really inspiring. I asked myself the questions: Can we leave thoughts behind? Can we leave problems behind? How do I deal with challenges before I let it go?" Leah from the USA was "able to let go of things I never was supposed to be holding on to. I could lighten my load and still survive moving forward. . . . My backpack was a metaphor for my responsibilities. I was able to sort out what was really not my responsibility or what I needed to be at peace with in my life." Wendy from Australia "was conscious at Cruz de Ferro that the stones laid around the cross were heavy with purpose and that so many of us had so many things that we needed to leave behind or rid ourselves of in order to carry on. And the stones represented that 'fear' or 'negativity' that we were leaving behind."

Deb from Australia shared this story about her Camino that struck me: "Why the Camino de Santiago? Nineteen months ago my husband left me. There were times I thought this is the end, I can't live without him. Then I heard about the walk of the Camino de Santiago in Europe and how you come back a changed person. So I thought it would get my ex out of my head and heart. I booked my flights and accommodation and waited six months, doing a lot of research and reading about personal experiences. It was then that I realized this journey was about *me*, not him. I had to prove to myself that I didn't need him or his approval. It was time to see what I could do on my own. This trip took me out of my comfort zone, and I had a fabulous time."

I started my own Camino as just another travel adventure. By the end, though, the Camino had this impact on me as well. The stone I left on that pile represented two pieces of baggage that had been weighing me down, both professionally and personally, for a couple of years. Only by dropping them did I realize how much they weighed.

HOW TO DO THIS AT WORK:

▸ *Claim Your Baggage*—We all have some baggage that weighs us down in our personal or professional lives: A bad habit we want to quit. A fear we've never confronted. A loss we can't get past. A toxic relationship we can't escape. Whatever your baggage is, the first step to dropping it is to identify it.

▸ *Weigh Your Baggage*—The next step is to assess how that baggage affects you and others. How does it shape your behavior? Are you hiding it? What do you do differently now than you did before you were weighed down with your baggage? How does that behavior affect your life and work? How does it affect those who need you at work and home?

▸ *Drop Off Your Baggage*—The best way to improve your leadership is to improve yourself as a person. Make a commitment to drop the stone you are carrying. Set a deadline. Define what success looks like.

▸ *Find Your Own Cruz de Ferro*—If you have unsuccessfully tried to drop your baggage, why not try an adventure like the Camino? The Camino is the most effective change agent I have experienced. I've never again seen the baggage I left on that pile.

PART IV

SHARING THE CAMINO

The Camino near Ganso, Spain.

CHAPTER 14

Find Your Own Camino

PILGRIMS BECOME AMBASSADORS FOR THE CAMINO UPON RETURNING
to the "real" world, encouraging others to do it. Terry, from
England, says, "Whenever I can, I share my experiences of the
Camino. . . . The Camino gave me a sense of purpose." Jodi,
from the USA, encourages others this way: "You can do it . . .
your mind is the biggest obstacle to tackle. You are stronger
than you can even imagine!" Maryanne, from the USA, shared
her story this way: "When people find out that I have walked
the Camino, they seem to be in awe of me, which makes me
laugh. Anyone can do it. You just have to really want to do it
and make the time for it." Stephen, from England, said, "People couldn't believe that I had done it, and it has prompted a
few friends to seriously think about doing it themselves. I also
believe that anybody of any age can do the Camino given the
time."

Not everyone can take a month off or walk fifteen miles a
day. Even if you can't do the Camino, there are ways to get the
same benefits by finding other ways to get the lessons the
Camino offers. These are the six features that make the Camino
a transformative adventure.

#1. *Alone Time for Self-Reflection*—A path like the Camino
provides plenty of easy-to-get alone time. If you want to get
away from other people, you can just slow down or speed up
and let others go by. With today's communication technology,
alone time also means turning off your mobile phone to avoid

distraction. Traveling through remote areas poorly served by phone coverage helps, by taking away the temptation to answer the phone. It also provides a good excuse for not being reachable at all times. Once you have alone time, you will find it much easier to self-reflect.

> Tip—Find adventures that disconnect you from work and life outside for hours at a time. Traveling and remote locations help with this. Other activities where distractions are not welcome—e.g., operating a motor vehicle—can be useful, too.

#2. Easy Interactions with Strangers—The Camino provides many opportunities to meet new people. Camino pilgrims meet each other every day on the trail, at food and water rest stops, at the sights along the way, and at the *albergues* each night. Each of these new interactions is the opportunity to have a conversation with someone with a very different background than your own.

> Tip—Find adventures that channel you into easy interactions with strangers. Transportation options like cruise ships or trains can be better than driving alone. Group trips can be a good option as well.

#3. Shared Challenges for Camaraderie—Overcoming the shared physical challenge of the Camino builds camaraderie between pilgrims. Within a few days on the Camino, every *peregrino* has "war stories" and tips to share that make connecting with other pilgrims easy. These stories and tips also help build camaraderie with pilgrims who have done the path before or who will do it in the future. This camaraderie makes the difference between feeling like you are *doing* something and feeling like you are *part* of something.

Tip—Find adventures that people do to pursue some shared interest. Shared interests in things like history, genealogy, sports teams, alumni groups, and others can provide a natural sense of camaraderie.

#4. *Charted Path of the Journey*—The Camino is very well marked all along the way. That frees pilgrims from monitoring maps and allows them to better experience the journey. Path markings don't just mean physical marks along the path, either. Guidebooks can provide invaluable maps and waymarks. They also indicate that enough other people do the experience to justify the existence of a guidebook.

Tip—Find adventures that are organized and well documented. If you can't find a guidebook or website about a potential adventure, rethink that as your adventure.

#5. *A Meaningful Achievement for Self-Confidence*—Walking the Camino for a month gives pilgrims an entry into an exclusive club—people who have walked across a large country. I've heard of people who have walked across the USA and been impressed, but never considered it myself because of the time commitment of several months. Find an adventure that sounds like an impressive feat that will help convince yourself that you can do impossible-sounding things if you set your mind on it.

Tip—Find adventures that have a beginning and ending context that sound like a big achievement. For example, walking across Spain sounds more meaningful than walking a different, random 800 kilometers in a month.

#6. *Transcendent Experience for Inspiration*—Many people do the Camino to find religious inspiration. Many find inspiration from the history. A good adventure should feature some form of inspiration you don't get in your everyday life. It could be stunning natural beauty, fascinating history, or personal family ties. Whatever it is, you should connect with your adventure in some deeper way to open you up to all the benefits.

Tip—Find adventures that transport you far away from your everyday existence.

The combination of all six of these features makes the Camino a transformative adventure. If you can't do the Camino, what other experiences can offer some, or all, of these features?

Do a Different Adventure You Can Do—If walking across a country is not for you, consider taking a cross-country trip in another way. You can drive, railroad, or bicycle. Maybe even take a boat. There are many ways to travel, and they all can include at least some of the above elements if you try.

Find Adventures Already in Your Life—Perhaps you are already living an adventure in part of your life and can focus on it. Things like parenting, taking care of loved ones, going back to school later in life, and reentering the workforce are all adventures people live every day. If you are on an adventure like this already, think about how you can draw out some of the six elements from that experience.

Camp on a Trail—Sometimes the way to experience a trail is to camp out on it and watch the adventure go by. Some people experience the Camino by volunteering to work in one of the *albergues* for a week or more. They meet many pilgrims from around the world without walking themselves. Volunteering in other places that serve people in need can also provide a transformative adventure.

If you are now thinking about doing an adventure like the Camino, there is one last thing you should know. Your adventure starts the day you start thinking about it. So let me be the first to say this to you—"Buen Camino!"

Epilogue

IF YOU CONSIDER THE CAMINO DE SANTIAGO TO BE AN ORGANIZA-
tion, it would be considered a success story equaled by few
other organizations. It is still thriving a thousand years after
its birth. How many other organizations around today—such
as cities, countries, or religions—are still thriving after a millennium? If the "Millennium Club" had an annual members'
meeting, the Camino would be among a very exclusive crowd.

On the surface, one reason for the success of the Camino has
been the clarity and consistency of its mission. The Camino
today serves the same purpose it did at its inception a thousand
years ago. It connects pilgrims from around the world to the
shrine to Saint James in the northwest corner of Spain. While
transportation technology has changed immensely over the last
thousand years, the Camino has not changed much.

Digging deeper, the secret to the Camino's success has been
its ability to meet a customer demand that has endured for centuries—pilgrimage. Pilgrimage has changed much over the centuries but has never gone away. At the Camino's beginning,
pilgrimage was about people pursuing a religious epiphany and
traveling by the means most available—by foot. Over time, the
journey itself started becoming part, or most, of the reward.
Tourism, adventure-seeking, self-discovery, and other urges became motivations for pilgrimage. By appealing to those needs,
the Camino found itself sitting on top of a well-diversified and

continually renewable source of customers. Chris from the USA summed it up like this: "One of the best things I heard on the Camino was from an Irish priest who told me that everyone asks each other why they are on the Camino, but they have it all wrong. The Camino chose them."

The Camino chose me, just as it has chosen millions of people through the centuries. It lured me with its tourism and adventure-seeking appeals to deliver the self-discovery it knew I needed.

Thank you for letting me share my Camino story with you. I hope you find your Camino . . . or that your Camino finds you.

Appendix A

What to Know If
You Want to Walk the Camino

IF THIS BOOK HAS YOU THINKING ABOUT WALKING THE CAMINO, THERE are better books than this to prepare you for the logistics. The Camino guidebook written by John Brierley seemed to be the most popular among pilgrims I walked with, at least those who prefer books in English. I used that book and highly recommend it. It gives you most everything you need to plan beforehand and to guide you while walking the Camino.

I *will* help you decide if it is worth investing in a Camino guidebook. I get questions from people who read about my Camino experience and are thinking about doing the Camino themselves. Typically, their biggest questions center on whether the Camino would even be possible for them. Here are the ten most frequent concerns I hear, and my responses.

1. "I can't walk that far."—People are often shocked to hear fifteen miles per day is a typical average on the Camino. That's like walking more than a half-marathon every day. The key is that pilgrims have all day to cover that distance. A typical person walks about three miles per hour, so an average Camino day would take about five hours at that pace. Even when you add time for breaks and a slower pace because of a backpack, you still have plenty of time each day as long as you start in the morning.

2. *"I can't take a month off."*—If you want to walk the whole Camino across Spain in one go, you need a month or more off. Many pilgrims do the Camino in parts, however, to get around this. Some do it one or two weeks at a time. Many just do the last hundred kilometers (sixty-two miles) into Santiago, which is the minimum distance needed to earn a Compostela certificate for a walker.

3. *"I can't afford it."*—Most people know whether they can afford the cost of airline or other travel to get to the Camino. What they don't know is whether they can afford to pay for hotels for a month. The secret to the Camino is that there are low-cost hostels available along the Camino that are only open to pilgrims. These hostels—*albergues*—typically charge a minimal price for sleeping space and meals tailored for a pilgrim budget. Some even offer free service to pilgrims who cannot pay. The trade-off is that these accommodations typically consist of nothing more than bunk bed in a shared room with shared bathrooms.

4. *"I can't speak Spanish."*—Like in most tourist-dependent parts of Western Europe, people serving tourists typically speak at least some English. Ironically, I speak Spanish but rarely had to use it because English was everywhere on the Camino. That wasn't because native English speakers made up a majority of pilgrims. It was because pilgrims came from many different countries with different languages. Because English is the most common second language, most conversa-

tions I heard between people from different countries were in English.

5. *"I'm not religious."*—The trail was started for religious reasons and still is closely associated with the Roman Catholic Church. Many of the major tourist sites are churches. However, there is no religious requirement or prohibition for being a Camino pilgrim. You can be from any religion or no religion. If you want to avoid religion, you can avoid going into churches. You can also avoid staying in the *albergues* that weave in prayers or religious services as part of the reason for their generously low prices. Your Camino can have as much or as little religion in it as you want. The only thing you need to do is to be thoughtful to respect others along the way, particularly pilgrims doing the Camino for religious reasons.

6. *"I can't travel alone."*—Many people do the Camino on their own. The structure of the Camino makes it different than doing a typical tourist vacation to Europe. Pilgrims form a community along the trail and generally look to help each other out. Those starting or ending at the same time form a loose cohort that sleeps and eats in the same places at the same times. The shared *peregrino* experience makes it easy to meet new people and form friendships.

7. *"I can't travel in groups."*—While the Camino can be a very social-group experience, it doesn't have to be. It is easy to be completely independent from other pilgrims if you want. It doesn't take much to avoid people. If you just speed up or slow down one day, you will be around an entirely new cohort of pilgrims.

8. *"I can't do the big climbs."*—For those starting in France, the

climb over the Pyrenees Mountains that form the border with Spain is a major hurdle right at the beginning. After that, there are a few days requiring big climbs. You can avoid doing those by starting after the Pyrenees (e.g., in Pamplona), by skipping sections, or by taking other forms of transportation. I started in Pamplona. There are trade-offs to each of those. You might feel like you are cutting corners and missing the full Camino experience. You might also fall behind or skip ahead of a cohort of fellow pilgrims. The only place you have to walk all the time is the last 100 kilometers if you want to be able to earn a Compostela certificate. If big climbs are going to hold you back from starting or finishing your Camino, do what you need to do. I don't regret my decision to skip the Pyrenees; that was part of my overall decision to be brave and start the Camino. I'll just do that stage in a future Camino.

9. *"I can't share accommodations with strangers."*—Most pilgrims stay at least one night in a hostel with communal sleeping and bathroom arrangements. Many do it to take advantage of the low cost. Others do it because it is part of the Camino experience. In some cases, there may be no alternative. Many pilgrims have never before shared accommodations on travel. They get past their pre-Camino mind-set about having a private room, so maybe you can, too. Personally, I admit I didn't. I reserved a private room in advance all along the way on my Camino. That was nice but it took a lot of work and it locked me into a rigid itinerary. My *peregrino* friends teased me about it and I missed out on that part of the Camino experience. But that was what it took me to be brave enough to start the Camino, so I wouldn't change it. On my next Camino, I will do the shared rooms at least part of the time.

10. *"I can't be out of reach."*—If you need to be on call 24/7 even

on vacation, the Camino is not for you. Most of the Camino is along remote countryside connecting small villages. If you are coming from overseas, you are probably several time zones apart from your home and office. You would also ruin your own Camino and likely annoy your fellow pilgrims if you worked while walking. But if you just need to check in periodically, you can. Wi-Fi is common at lunch and evening rest stops. If you have to be connected to work more than that while on vacation, I would suggest you focus on the "why" versus "how" question when planning your next vacation.

If you are still thinking about doing the Camino, here are some suggestions to help you further focus your planning.

▸ *When to start*—Timing your Camino is a lot like timing any vacation to Europe. The summer months are the most crowded and hottest. August, in particular, is worth avoiding if possible. Winters are worth avoiding, too. The weather can be cold and even dangerous, particularly in the mountains and high elevations. You will not meet many fellow pilgrims. Some *albergues* close for the season, too. The fall is probably the best time to go. The weather is typically milder. The trail is busy enough for things to be open, and you will have other pilgrims to meet. Late spring can work well, too.

▸ *Which trail to do*—The Camino has many different routes across Spain, depending on where they start. The most popular trail by far is the French Route (Camino Frances), which crosses northern Spain in an arc connecting Pamplona, Burgos, and Leon on the way to Santiago. St. Jean Pied-de-Port, on the French side of the Pyrenees, is the traditional starting point. There are other trails as well that are less busy and more sparse in terms of places to stay and eat. Like a typical first-timer on the Camino, I chose the French Route for my first Camino, but plan to do the Portuguese Route next.

▶ *Where to start*—Deciding where to start depends on the length of your trip and your goal. If you want to end in Santiago and get a Compostela, and you only have a week, you should probably start around Sarria. The trail is at its busiest from there on, with many groups starting there, particularly Spaniards. For people who have been walking for weeks before, the surge in traffic can be an unpleasant change. If you only have a week and just want to do the best part of the trip, I would suggest the week before Sarria or the first week starting in St. Jean Pied-de-Port. That avoids much of the flat plain of the meseta, which is the least scenic part of the trail. If you do have a whole month, starting in St. Jean Pied-de-Port will give you the "full per-egrino experience" by crossing the Pyrenees.

▶ *How to plan*—Ironically, a monthlong vacation takes a lot of work to set up. The best way to start is to make a few choices on the main options around a Camino. First, you can do the Camino on your own or you can go with a group. There are many travel companies that organize trips and make all the arrangements. If you are willing to pay for the service, a group trip can be a good way to convince yourself to go. The next big decision is about your airfare. You can book your round trip and lock in your days. Another option is booking your travel as two one-way tickets, which can give you more flexibility. The final big decision is whether to have reservations for overnight accommodations. Doing so takes a lot of work and locks you in to an itinerary, but it can remove the stress some pilgrims face at the busy seasons when some *albergues* get full.

I hope that helps. Buen Camino!

Appendix B

The Camino Today

HOW MANY PILGRIMS DO THE CAMINO? THE CATHEDRAL IN SANTIAGO has been keeping statistics since 1986 on the number of pilgrims completing the Camino and getting a Compostela certificate. The total number of Compostelas issued has risen steadily from 2,491 in 1986 to 262,458 in 2015.[1] Once every five years or so, when there is a Holy Year, the number of pilgrims spikes dramatically, but then it returns to normal growth the following year.

How many pilgrims have done the Camino? Since 1986, 2.8 million Compostelas have been issued to Camino pilgrims completing at least the last 100 kilometers of the trail on foot (or 200 kilometers on bicycle).[2] Ninety percent of pilgrims who earned a Compostela in 2015 did it on foot, with the rest doing it by bicycle.[3] Half of those Compostelas were offered in just the last seven years of that thirty-year period.

Where are today's pilgrims from? The nationality of Compostela recipients today is about evenly split between Spanish and non-Spanish, with foreigners taking a slight but growing majority since 2012.[4] Most of the non-Spanish pilgrims come from other countries in Europe.

How many US citizens do the Camino? Pilgrims from the USA account for a small, but growing, share. Since the US film

The Way came out in 2010, the US share of Compostelas has averaged about 2.5 percent of the total, up from 0.8 percent of the total before that.[5] If you assume that 0.8 percent of the 1,039,102 Compostelas issued from 1986 to 2006 went to US pilgrims, that would mean that roughly 8,000 Compostelas issued during that period went to US citizens.[6] In the 2007–2015 period when statistics by country were collected, 27,569 Compostelas went to US citizens.[7] All told, that means that an estimated 35,000 Compostelas went to Americans from 1986 to 2015. With a population of over 300 million in the USA, that means that perhaps about 1 in 10,000 US citizens had earned a Compostela through 2015.[8] US presence on the Camino continues to grow rapidly, increasing from about 2 percent in 2011 to 5.2 percent in 2015.[9]

Who are today's pilgrims? The Compostela recipients are about equally split between men and women, although that is only after a faster climb in women's participation since the early 1990s, when men outnumbered women by about 2 to 1.[10] About 55 percent of Compostelas went to people between the ages of 30 and 60 over the last decade, about 30 percent went to people under 30, and about 15 percent to people over 60.[11] In 2015, 19 percent of Compostelas went to people who identified their occupation as "students," 12 percent were "retired," and the rest were sprinkled across a variety of other occupations. Many of these students were likely part of group trips from schools in Spain.

What is the reason for today's pilgrims to do the Camino? About 40 percent of pilgrims earning a Compostela over the last ten years have chosen "Religious" as their motivation for their Camino. Five to nine percent over that time have chosen "Cultural," with the rest saying it was some mix of the two.[12]

Sources

American Pilgrims on the Camino, 120 State Avenue NE #303, Olympia, WA 98501. www.americanpilgrims.org.

Camino Society Ireland. 36 Upper Baggot Street, Dublin 4. D04 R6Y6. Ireland. www.caminosociety.ie.

Gitlitz, David M., and Linda Kay Davidson. *The Pilgrimage Road to Santiago: The Complete Cultural Handbook. Kindle Edition.* New York: St. Martin's Griffin, 2000.

John Adams autobiography. Part 3. "Peace," 1779–1780. Sheet 11 of 18. 28 December 1779–6 January 1780. http://www.masshist.org/digitaladams/archive/doc, retrieved 8 November 2016.

Kreutz, Barbara. *Before the Normans: Southern Italy in the Ninth and Tenth Centuries. Kindle Version. University of Pennsylvania Press, 1996.*

Laffi, Domenico. *A Journey to the West: The Diary of a Seventeenth-Century Pilgrim from Bologna to Santiago de Compostela; Translated, with a Commentary by James Hall.* Published in 1997 by Primavera Pers. Leiden. The Netherlands & Conselleria de Cultura e Comunicacion Social, Xerencia de Promocion do Camino de Santiago.

The Pilgrimage to Compostela in the Middle Ages. Edited by Maryjane Dunn and Linda Davidson. New York and London: Routledge.

Pilgrim's Reception Office (*Oficina de Acogida al Peregrino*). Cathedral of Santiago. Rúa Carretas, n°33. 15705 Santiago de Compostela. A Coruña—ESPAÑA. www.oficinadelperegrino.com

Storrs, Constance Mary. *Jacobean Pilgrims from England to St. James of Compostela: From the Early Twelfth to the Late Fifteenth Century.* Confraternity of Saint James, 1998.

Webb, Diana. *Medieval European Pilgrimage, c. 700–c.1500.* New York: Palgrave, 2002.

Notes

Chapter 1

1 Storrs, Constance Mary. *Jacobean Pilgrims From England to St. James of Compostela: From the Early Twelfth to the Late Fifteenth Century.* Confraternity of Saint James, 1998, pp. 32–33.

2 I like the perspective that Maryjane, a professor from the USA, has about the story about St. James's remains: "If persons have no concept of who St. James was, and why the pilgrimage developed, then they could just as well walk the Appalachian Trail. You don't have to 'believe' in the efficacy of pilgrimage, or in the bones of the saint actually being there, but for goodness sake give some thought to what you're doing, and why others have done it."

3 Storrs, p. 33.

4 *The Pilgrimage to Compostela in the Middle Ages.* Edited by Maryjane Dunn and Linda Davidson. New York and London: Routledge, p. xxiv.

5 Webb, Diana. *Medieval European Pilgrimage, c. 700–c.1500.* New York: Palgrave, 2002, pp. 3–4.

6 Webb, p. 1.

7 Webb, p. 3.

8 Webb, p. 11.

9 Webb, p. 12.

10 Webb, p. 12.

11 Webb, p. 12.

12 Kreutz, Barbara. *Before the Normans: Southern Italy in the Ninth and Tenth Centuries.* University of Pennsylvania Press 1996, Kindle version, location 821 of 5733.

13 Kreutz, location 816 of 5733.

14 Storrs, p. 33.

15 Storrs, p. 32.

16 Webb, p. 13.

17 Webb, p. 13.

18 Storrs, p. 33.

19 Storrs, p. 34.

20 Storrs, p. 35.

21 Storrs, p. 37.

22 Storrs, pp. 39–40.

23 Webb, p. 23.

24 Webb, p. 24.

25 Webb, p. 35.

26 Storrs, p. 42.

27 Dunn and Davidson, p. xxvii.

28 Storrs, p. 46.

29 Storrs, p. 42.

30 Storrs, p. 57.

31 Storrs, p. 56.

32 Storrs, p. 60.

33 Laffi, Domenico. *A Journey to the West: The Diary of a Seventeenth-Century Pilgrim from Bologna to Santiago de Compostela;* Translated, with a Commentary by James Hall. Published 1997 by Primavera Pers. Leiden. The Netherlands & Conselleria de Cultura e Comunication Social, Xerencia de Promocion do Camino de Santiago, p. 113.

34 Gitlitz and Davidson, location 4710 of 11301.

35 Dunn and Davidson, pp. xxvi–xxvii.

36 OficinaDelPeregrino.com/en/statistics, retrieved July 27, 2016.

37 Gitlitz and Davidson, location 7475 of 11302.

38 Webb, p. 42.

39 Gitlitz and Davidson, location 7475 of 11302.

40 Gitlitz and Davidson, location 7475 of 11302.

41 John Adams autobiography. Part 3. "Peace," 1779–1780. Sheet 11 of 18. 28 December 1779–6 January 1780. http://www.masshist.org/digitaladams/archive/doc, retrieved 8 November 2016.

42 Dunn and Davidson, p. xxxiii.

43 Dunn and Davidson, p. xxxiii.

44 Dunn and Davidson, p. xxxiv.

45 http://www.americanpilgrims.org/assets/media/statistics/apoc_redentials_by_year_07-15.pdf, retrieved 6 October 2015.

46 https://oficinadelperegrino.com/en/statistics/, retrieved July 21, 2016.

Chapter 3

1 Gitlitz, David M. and Linda Kay Davidson. *The Pilgrimage Road to Santiago: The Complete Cultural Handbook*. Kindle Edition. New York. St. Martin's Griffin. 2000. Location 3898 of 11301.
2 Laffi, p. 151. Quote used with permission.

Chapter 8

1 http://www.caminosociety.ie/caminos/beatitudes.403.html, retrieved November 9, 2016.

Chapter 9

1 Laffi, p. 142. Quote used with permission.
2 "Brokaw Addresses Graduates' Futures." *The Summer Pennsylvanian*, May 23, 1996, p. 3. http://www.library.upenn.edu/docs/kislak/dp/1996/1996_05_23.pdf, retrieved 29 October 2016.

Chapter 13

1 https://oficinadelperegrino.com/en/statistics/, retrieved November 9, 2016.

Appendix B

1 http://www.americanpilgrims.org/assets/media/statistics/compostelas_by_year_86-15.pdf, retrieved November 9, 2016.
2 http://www.americanpilgrims.org/assets/media/statistics/compostelas_by_year_86-15.pdf, retrieved November 9, 2016.
3 https://oficinadelperegrino.com/en/statistics/, retrieved October 6, 2016.
4 https://oficinadelperegrino.com/en/statistics/, retrieved October 6, 2016.
5 http://www.americanpilgrims.org/assets/media/statistics/apoc_credentials_by_year_07-15.pdf, retrieved October 7, 2016.
6 http://www.americanpilgrims.org/assets/media/statistics/apoc_credentials_by_year_07-15.pdf, retrieved October 7, 2016.

7   http://www.americanpilgrims.org/assets/media/statistics/apoc_
     credentials_by_year_07-15.pdf, retrieved October 7, 2016.

8   http://www.americanpilgrims.org/assets/media/statistics/apoc_
     credentials_by_year_07-15.pdf, retrieved October 7, 2016.

9   http://www.americanpilgrims.org/assets/media/statistics/us_per-
     cent_total_compostelas_07-15.pdf, retrieved October 6, 2016.

10   http://www.americanpilgrims.org/assets/media/statistics/compos-
     telas_by_sex_91-15.pdf, retrieved October 6, 2016.

11   http://www.americanpilgrims.org/assets/media/statistics/compos-
     telas_by_age_06-15.pdf, retrieved October 6, 2016.

12   https://oficinadelperegrino.com/en/statistics/, retrieved October 6,
     2016.

Index